Gods of Rome

Gods of Rome

A Primer for Young Adults

Clara Tagliacozzo-Lee

Columbus, Ohio

The views and opinions expressed in this book are solely those of the author and do not reflect the views or opinions of Gatekeeper Press. Gatekeeper Press is not to be held responsible for and expressly disclaims responsibility of the content herein.

Gods of Rome: A Primer for Young Adults

Published by Gatekeeper Press
2167 Stringtown Rd, Suite 109
Columbus, OH 43123-2989
www.GatekeeperPress.com

Copyright © 2021 by Clara Tagliacozzo-Lee
All rights reserved. Neither this book, nor any parts within it may be sold or reproduced in any form or by any electronic or mechanical means, including information storage and retrieval systems, without permission in writing from the author. The only exception is by a reviewer, who may quote short excerpts in a review.

The cover design, interior formatting, typesetting, and editorial work for this book are entirely the product of the author. Gatekeeper Press did not participate in and is not responsible for any aspect of these elements.

ISBN (paperback): 9781662915543

Table of Contents

Introduction   1
Figure 1: Table of Roman and Greek God Equivalencies   4
Figure 2: Map of the Roman World   7

Gods

Jupiter	10
Juno	12
Diana	14
Victoria	16
Pax	18
Pluto	20
Nemesis	22
Venus	24
Caelestis	26
Minerva as Warrior	28
Minerva and Wisdom	30
Neptune	32
Fortuna	34
Sol	36
Ulysses	38
Saturn	40
Aglibol and Malakbel	42
Terminus	44
Salus	46
Polyphemus as Lover	48
Polyphemus as Monster	50
Vulcan	52
Vesta	54

Ceres	56
Bacchus	58
Folk Understandings and Prayers	60
Iris	62
Proserpina	64
Mars as Soldier	66
Mars as Paramour	68
Medusa	70
Somnus	72
Tellus	74
Fides	76
Hercules as Hero	78
Hercules as Deity	80
Nyx	82
Venti	84
Apollo	86
Mercury	88
Asclepius	90
Pan	92
Cloacina	94
Janus	96
Luna	98
Cupid	100
Moses	102
Jesus	104
Saint Sebastian	106
Saint Emerenziana (Christian Sister of St. Agnes)	108
Figure 3: Roman Emperor Timeline	110
Works Consulted and Further Reading:	111

Introduction

My dad's family is from Italy and my mom's family is from Taiwan. My heritage was therefore one key factor in my decision to pursue the project of writing this book. I have always been in love with the gods of Rome. This was partially based on my family, as I said; but it was also partially based on my discovery of the Percy Jackson series, and all the subsequent books, written by Rick Riordan. These are books oriented toward young adults and were especially popular when I started high school, which is when I first came up with the idea of this project, to share my love for the subject. As a young woman, the gods who were supposed to interest me most were Venus, Diana and Vesta, perhaps. But in reality, my attention was most focused on Jupiter, Minerva and Mars. The inherent difference in Ares vs. Mars, for example, really intrigued me (his Greek manifestation vs. his Roman one). How do we know what the gods were really like? How do we know what Romans really thought about them? Why were some more important than others? Which are the ones that last? These are the kinds of questions that I had as I was getting older, and growing up.

I have been to Europe just once in my life, on a family trip. This was only possible became we have family in Italy, which made the costs manageable. I took that time to visit museums and delve deeper into my growing interest in writing this book, which I had been thinking about for a while. This trip was especially memorable because I got to meet many of the family members I described above for the first time. Our first destination was to London, where I got to visit the British Museum. Some of the gods described here are from that institution. But most of the photos and descriptions here were from various museums and archaeological sites we visited in Rome. Seeing as it was my first time there, I went to the Colosseum and the Pantheon and other famous buildings. But I really spent a lot of time tracking down gods, through various museums and sites across the capitol. These included the inter-locking complex of museums known as the Capital Line Museum, but also St. Agnes' Church, the Palazzo Massimo, and other venues. I spent a lot of time on my feet, moving between gods, and taking lots of pictures. Later when I came back to the United States I spent more time doing research on the gods, and confirming knowledge that was partly in my head about all of these vanished deities. Being able to take this trip made me realize how exciting and meaningful the Roman gods have become to me, initially through Rick Riordan and these teenage books, but increasingly through my hours of research and writing, and seeing these artworks in person, and through the lens of a camera.

This book looks at fifty different gods. I touch upon all of the most famous gods most everyone has heard of, including Jupiter, Neptune, Mars, Venus, and the like. These gods are the most well-known because they have the most important functions, both in mythology and during the life of the Roman Empire. While most of my knowledge was centered around these "major gods", I also incorporated minor gods, which required extra research but which was more fun, on the whole, because I knew less about them. So, in addition to Jupiter, Neptune, and others, I also include material on Janus, the god of choices (and doors); Ceres, the goddess of the harvest; and even Vesta, the virgin goddess of the hearth. But I didn't stop there. Many of the museums that I visited also had non-Roman deities on display, a whole new category of beings to research. I was immediately intrigued, and began trying to find connections and parallels between these new legends and the ones I already knew. In this category I would put gods like Aglibol and Malakbel, two gods who originated in Syria but who became relevant to the Roman Empire during the third century CE. Also important in this sense were Jesus, Moses, and other saints of the Christian and Jewish traditions, who were worshipped by minorities during the height of the Roman Empire.

One of the unique things about doing this project was seeing how each work of art was crafted, as all of them had origins in different time periods, and different parts of the ancient world. For example, though we may not know the exact artist of every piece, we know the approximate time-period each object was made, and sometimes the provenance can be narrowed down to a specific year, or series of years. We also know something about the artists who made the artworks themselves. All of the pieces shown here were made from different materials, and by different classes of artists. So, for example, these included marble statues and busts, which were the most common in the Roman tradition. But we also see later renditions of the gods in oil paintings, some of which can be very beautiful (and even can look rather modern). There are also several instances of stone mosaics, which reiterates the lived-approach to art in the ancient Roman Empire. A pair of bronze hands shows us that the medium of expression greatly varied throughout the time periods of Rome. That diversity of construction made this project all the more interesting and aesthetically pleasing to me as an observer. It was also clear that the Romans owed a lot to the Greeks, since the Greek tradition in both art and religion were mirrored in Roman times. Sometimes, this was not true, however. The Greeks worshipped Poseidon far more than the Romans worshipped Neptune, as the Romans were more fearful of sea-travel on the whole than their Greek predecessors. Mars in Rome, however, was far more important than Ares was in Greece.

Greek Name	Roman Name	Domain	Other Names/ Symbols	Traits (Personal/ Physical)	Significant Family Ties
Zeus	Jupiter/ Jove	Supreme Ruler; Lord of the Sky; Rain God	God of gods *lightning bolt, eagle, oak tree	Power greater than all divinities combined; philanderer	Married to Hera; gave birth to Athena out of his head
Hera	Juno	Protector of marriage	*cow, peacock	Jealous, vengeful, protector of heroes	Zeus's sister and wife
Poseidon	Neptune	Ruler of the Sea	Earth Shaker *trident, bull, horse	Always carried trident; second in eminence to Zeus	Zeus's brother; married to Amphitrite
Hades	Pluto	Ruler of the Underworld	God of Wealth, King of the Dead	Wears helmet of invisibility; unpitying but just	Married to Persephone; brother of Zeus Poseidon, etc.
Pallas Athena	Minerva	Goddess of the city; organized life and culture	Maiden of the Parthenon temple *owl, olive tree	Virgin battle goddess; ruthless, wise and pure; dressed in armor	Daughter of Zeus; no mother
Phoebus Apollo	Phoebus Apollo	God of archery, music, healing, truth and light	The most Greek god *dolphin, crow, laurel tree	Honest, true; carries golden lyre	Son of Zeus and Leto; twin brother of Artemis
Artemis	Diana	Goddess of wild things, the moon, the hunt; protectress of youth	Cynthia *moon, deer, cypress	Virgin goddess; Fierce and vengeful	Daughter of Zeus and Leto; Apollo's twin sister
Aphrodite	Venus	Goddess of Love and Beauty	*dove, roses, swan, sparrow, myrtle	Most beautiful of all the gods, laughing	Daughter of Zeus and Dione (or born from foam of sea); married to Hephaestus
Hermes	Mercury	Zeus's messenger, herald; protector of traders	God of commerce and Thieves *winged sandals/helmet, Caduceus	Master Thief; shrewd, cunning, graceful and swift	Son of Zeus and Maia
Ares	Mars	God of War	*shining armor, vulture, dog	Hateful, violent, cowardly, ruthless, murderous	Son of Zeus and Hera
Hephaestus	Vulcan/ Mulciber	God of Fire and the Forge	Protector of Smiths *volcano	Ugly, lame, peace-loving, kindly	Son of Zeus and Hera; married to Aphrodite
Hestia	Vesta	Goddess of the Home/Hearth	*hearth	Virgin goddess	Sister of Zeus

Figure 1: Table of Roman and Greek God Equivalencies

Readers of this book will see some gods who are very familiar to them. These include Jupiter, the king of the gods, who was the main god of Rome and the ruler of what was deemed the most important realm of existence: the sky. Also portrayed is Mars, god of war and Jupiter's right-hand man, as the father of Romulus and Remus, the brothers who founded the city of Rome in antiquity. He was considered second only to Jupiter because of his connections to Rome itself. Pluto, one of Jupiter's brothers, ruled over another realm of existence: the underworld. Similar to the Greeks, the Romans did not fear death, but rather were steady in their belief that there was an afterlife. A fourth main god I highlight here is Juno, the wife of Jupiter and thus the queen of all the gods. Her domain focused on women in general: the protection of women, marriage and fertility – all of which were respected and worshipped during this time. A fifth and final major god was Mercury, the god of trade, messages, and travel. Mercury is most notable for his occupation as the messenger of the gods, which makes him relevant in many mythologies and stories where the gods come into contact with mortals. All of these important deities played a vital role in the pantheon of Rome's religion, and were among the most worshipped and respected gods. For this reason, I have only been able to include limited examples of them, despite their prevalence in the artwork I saw.

These are some of the main gods, but over the course of this project, I tried to branch out in my knowledge, and incorporate some of the hundreds of other gods who Romans worshipped. For example, Vesta is important because she was the goddess of the family, home, and hearth. Thus Romans respected her because of their loyalty to the community, which she represented. Fortuna was also interesting to research, as she was the goddess of luck and fortune, and is known in mythology for her horn of plenty, which was later developed into the cornucopia (which later again developed into American ideas of Thanksgiving, and the notion of plenty). Terminus was also fascinating to me, because of his specific domain of boundaries and boundary stones. He showed that property and notions of ownership of the land were increasingly important in ancient Rome as it developed into a more sophisticated society. The goddess Nemesis was considered a more minor god despite her prevalence in Roman lore. Given the omnipresence of Roman warfare, her specialties in revenge and retribution were idolized and made use of on a regular basis. So one can see that these lesser-known gods were important in their own way, and very visible across Roman society, including across economic classes.

However, when I was at these museums and archaeological sites, I stumbled upon artworks depicting non-Roman religions and beliefs as well. I realized that I could also include and connect them to my project, and their relevance in the Roman pantheon of ideas. In this category I would put the bronze arms seen in this book, which were made during Caligula's reign of terror, and which represent everyday beliefs which point not to an individual god or goddess, but to a general higher being, sought-after for the purpose of warding off evil. The image of Moses that I have included shows that Jews were part of the Roman empire too, both of their own accord and as they were represented by Roman and non-Roman artists. Jesus also makes an appearance in these pages, as his sculpture was a prevalent figure in the pantheon of wider images of Rome at this time. It was unknown two thousand years ago that Jesus would become the figurehead of a global, worldwide religion. The adoption of Christianity by parts of Rome's people initiated a new move toward monotheism, and away from the wider Roman pantheon of gods. However, saint-worship itself was a form of polytheism in that Romans prayed to and idolized people like Saint Sebastian and Saint Emerenziana, two figures I highlight in this book. Even though they were not necessarily traditional deities in Roman mythology, these saints still proved to be an essential part of Roman religious life toward the end of the empire.

Figure 2: Map of the Roman World

Why should we care about gods that existed and were worshipped two thousand years ago? The simple fact that so many modern people have read the *Odyssey*, the *Illiad*, and other books from antiquity, and taken the time to study and revive ancient history, just goes to show how relevant these ideologies still are today. Personally, the fantastic writing and story-telling of the Percy Jackson books brought these characters and figures to life, not just for me, but for a whole generation of young adult readers. Though religion has evolved and developed into many forms, represented by many different sects, Graeco-Roman religion still echoes well in our time. Its common themes of protection from evil, fear of nature, and worry about the afterlife all still live in us now as modern human beings. Just as history teaches us not to repeat the mistakes of the past, the study of ancient religions helps to identify and trace the origins of our thought processes. The concerns highlighted in this book show us our most innate desires and beliefs about the world that surrounds us. In this we are no different than our Roman predecessors. Their concerns are our concerns, even if our beliefs have shifted to fit more modern circumstances.

Jupiter
Palazzo Massimo Museum
Rome, Italy
Date Unknown

Jupiter was the Roman king of the gods. His Greek counterpart was Zeus. Until Christianity took over as the main religion of the empire, Jupiter was the main god of Rome. As the god of the sky, which included thunder and lightning, he is characterized by his confident stature, and master lightning-bolts, which he wielded as a weapon. Throughout mythology, Jupiter was often characterized as the "biggest god" in the room. He was often depicted as a middle-aged man (with a full beard), and he held his lightning bolts in one hand, and a staff with an eagle on it in the other. He was always wearing regal clothing. As one of the "big three", his brothers Neptune and Pluto were gods of the realm of existence: the sky, the sea, and the underworld. These brothers were the most powerful gods, and sons of the Titan Saturn. As the most powerful god, he was honored and memorialized with the biggest and best temples, statues, and relics. One of the biggest temples of Jupiter was on Capitoline Hill in Rome itself. Within these temples, there were important scrolls and texts, and many statues of this prominent deity. Everyone came to pray in these temples: the poorest and the richest alike. War generals prayed and led their armies to such temples after a battle to commemorate victories. The people's feelings about Jupiter evolved as the life of the Roman Empire went on. During the period of time when the Romans were ruled by all-powerful emperors, the emperors made it clear to their populations that they, themselves, were the children of Jupiter. After Rome became a republic, Jupiter's role in society evolved to represent competing factions, either royal power or forbidden divine rights. Before, Rome had been ruled by emperors, who believed they were granted their power by Jupiter. However, once Rome became a republic, there were now two schools of thought. People either believed that Rome should return to the era of emperors and divine rights, or they believed that Rome was better ruled through multiple centers of power, all staffed by human beings (but with the gods above them). Jupiter and his image, in this way, was representative of the problems facing Rome generally in regard to politics: should they allow themselves to be ruled by one, or should many take part in the governance of the empire? The Romans thought that if only one person ruled, dictatorship was much too easy to achieve. Rule by many was messier, but could include more people's voices and represent more perspectives and the stratification of class in society.

Juno

Palazzo Massimo Museum
Rome, Italy
2nd Century AD

This feminine figure can be identified as the goddess of marriage and the queen of the gods, Juno (or Hera in Greece). The statue is wearing a *peplos* and its arms, now lost, were made separately. Alongside being the goddess of marriage, Juno was known for her patronage of childbirth, homemaking, and motherhood generally, thus making her a very important deity among the women of Rome. Moreover, not only was she the queen of the gods, and husband to Jupiter, she was one of the three Capitoline Hill "triad gods", along with Jupiter and Minerva. Much like many other gods, there was a difference between her Greek and Roman counterparts and these differences were depicted accordingly. Hera was generally depicted as more warm and motherly, while Juno was portrayed as more battle-ready, and was often carrying a spear and shield. However, both forms projected a majestic and powerful appearance, parallel to her standing amongst the gods. The cow was most often associated with Juno, and many portrayals of the goddess throughout history show Juno riding in a golden chariot pulled by peacocks. As the wife of Jupiter, she had two divine children, Mars and Vulcan. However, Juno was renowned for her all-consuming jealousy for her husband's many affairs with immortals and mortals alike. Many stories recall different versions of how Juno would torment her husband's mistresses, and how she would get revenge on Jupiter himself. She was also important in Roman festivals, and had a day dedicated to her, March 1st. On this day, it was tradition for husbands to shower their wives in gifts. There were two contradictory origins to this festival. Some say it was in honor of Mars' birthday, while others said that the festival honored the end of the Roman/Sabine war. It was said that women on opposing sides banded together and threw themselves between the two sets of combatants in order to achieve peace, and to end the war. The first of every month was also dedicated to Juno, and the month of June was named after the goddess. For such an important goddess, there are not many myths and stories where she is heavily featured, exposing her role as being somewhat subordinate to her husband. This could help explain the foundation of Juno's reputation as a petty, jealousy-driven goddess, one who was less important in many ways than Jupiter.

Diana

Palazzo Massimo Museum
Rome, Italy
2nd century AD

Diana was the goddess of the moon and the hunt. She is the daughter of Jupiter and a titan named Leto. Diana is most famous for her association with a group of hunters known as the "Hunters of Diana". This group of hunters were composed of solely female demigods and other supernatural beings who all took a vow of chastity, and worshipped Diana. They were often hired by the gods to track or kill dangerous monsters that had escaped, and they were known to be immortal after they joined the group. Diana herself was the goddess of childbirth, fertility, chastity and wild animals, as well as the hunt and the moon. Like many other gods, she was said to be able to both transform and also talk to animals, and could even control their behavior. The *Artemide Tipo Colonna* portrays the goddess Diana in the guise of a huntress with a bow, arrows, and a quiver, of which the quiver is the only strap to have survived. She was characterized to always carry her silver bow and arrow, and present herself as a young woman (from age ten to eighteen). As a goddess of chastity, she and Minerva and Vesta formed a triad of goddesses who swore that they would not marry. However, many mythologies recount that there were demigods born from the wisdom and hearth goddesses, but Diana was known to have taken the vow most seriously. She did not have any lovers or partners at all. As such, one of the most famous tales regarding Diana was that of her only romantic partner, the giant Orion. It was said that the huntsman was the only one to have ever won her heart, and he was allowed to join the Hunters of Diana. However, when Diana realized her mistake, and later ended their relationship, Orion slowly became bitter and distant, and eventually disappeared altogether. Different tales say different things, but the general consensus was that before Orion left the group, he and Artemis had a falling-out, and it was suspected that Artemis had shot and killed Orion. The other possibility was that Diana's twin brother, Apollo, disapproved of his sister breaking her vow, and set up a contest in which Diana unknowingly shot Orion in the head. When she realized what she had done, she used her power to turn the ashes of the dead giant into a constellation in the sky. Even to this day people who identify as "pagan" celebrate Diana on August 13th, when they pray to her to protect their harvests.

Victoria

Palazzo Massimo Museum
Rome, Italy
2nd century BCE

The goddess of victory is depicted here as a nude woman entwined in a golden, billowing fabric which she grasps in her hands. Aquamarine colored plumage adorns her beautiful wings, marking the woman to be of divine heritage. As the goddess of speed and strength as well as victory, it was fitting that she was characterized by her wings, and thus was nicknamed the "winged goddess". This winged characteristic was especially unique because while many gods were said to be able to transform a winged animal to fly around, Victoria was the only goddess who actually had wings. Ancient Greeks and Romans alike worshipped Victoria/Nike as they believed she could lead them to victory in battle, and grant strength and speed. She is also often associated with being the king of the Gods' chariot driver, and is often depicted as being seated near Jupiter himself. Moreover, many sculptures of prominent gods such as Jupiter and Minerva depict a small statue of Victoria in their right hand, symbolizing their power and strength, especially on the battlefield. The goddess was also commonly shown grasping a palm branch in her right hand as a symbol of peace, as well as wearing a wreath, so that she could crown a winner in any contest or battle. She was also considered a messenger for the gods, much like Mercury. She is most remembered for her role in the Titan War, in which she stayed by Jupiter's side and supposedly guaranteed the victory of the gods. Victoria was a child of Pallas, a Titan, and Styx, a goddess of a powerful river in the Underworld. She had three famous brothers: Zelos, the god of rivalry; Kratos, the god of strength; and Bia, the god of force. She and her siblings were brought to Jupiter by their mother to work for him. Victoria/Nike is still relevant today as a symbol in the Olympic games, vis-a-vis her torch, the wreath, etc. Many companies also pay tribute to the goddess in their logos and designs. The most famous example here of course is the multi-billion dollar conglomerate Nike, which manufactures shoes and clothing all over the world. The most famous sculpture of the goddess is not actually presented in Rome or Greece, but in the Louvre in Paris. Known as the "Winged Victory of Samothrace", it shows the goddess standing at the bow of a ship, presumably to showcase her confidence in the battle ahead. This is one of the most famous and well-known statues in the entire museum.

Pax

Museo dell'Ara Pacis
Rome, Italy
9 BCE

Pax was yet another daughter of Jupiter, and a goddess of justice named Justitia, and was a minor Roman goddess who was most prominent during the reign of the Roman emperor Augustus. As the goddess of peace, she is often depicted in artwork holding a cornucopia and an olive branch. The olive branch symbolized peace and serenity, while the cornucopia emphasized her connections to plenty, a good harvest, and bounty and prosperity. These symbols also suggested that there was more than enough peace available, if humans truly wanted to find it (Pax literally means "peace' in Latin). The Roman foundation for the word peace was derived from "pacisci", which can be translated in English as the word "pact". This represents Pax's connection to the end of a war, and the formation of an alliance and the start of peace. Though a minor goddess, an important festival was dedicated to her, known as the "Festival of Pax". This day was normally celebrated on January 3rd of each year. On this specific day, it was custom for Romans to place images of all of their leaders at the feet of a statue of the goddess. Most notably, she was recognized by the Roman emperors Augustus and Vespasian when they used her image on coins to honor her. She was nonetheless popular among the commoners of Rome when they prayed to her for self-understanding, and self-acceptance. She is generally associated with springtime, and has a temple called Ara Pacis on the Campus Martius in Rome. The monument itself was first erected on July 4th, 13 BCE to honor the Emperor Augustus, after being commissioned by the Roman senate. The Ara Pacis still stands today in Rome, after being rebuilt. Surprisingly, even though Pax was a minor goddess she had many other temples dedicated to her across the Roman Empire. These included an altar in Athens, and a temple on the Forum Pacis which was built in 75 CE. Pax was relatively ignored as a goddess because she had less significance in Roman philosophy as opposed to Greek thought. However, she was revived after her Greek equivalent, Eirene, rose in prominence during the Peloponnesian Wars. Peace was often viewed in Roman philosophy as the result of a war, not the non-presence of war itself.

Pluto
Detroit Institute of Arts
Detroit, MI
1545 CE

The sixteenth century German painter Hans Sebald Beham made this print of Hercules as he descended into the realm of the god Pluto, the underworld. He was bringing back Cerberus, the three-headed dog who vigilantly guards the mortal entrance to the land of the dead. Pluto finally agreed to let Hercules take Cerberus so long as he made no use of weapons in his quest. In this depiction of the story, Hercules put down his chosen weapon of a club, taking up instead three leashes to help him drag Cerberus from the fires of the underworld. Beham was one of a number of German printmakers now referred to as the "Little Masters." They established their artistic reputations by engraving extremely small prints, and these found favor with collectors who were fascinated by miniatures and curiosities. As one of the six children of the titan Saturn and Rhea, Pluto and his siblings overthrew their parents, and became the first ruling gods of Olympus. He and two of his brothers, Jupiter and Neptune, comprised the "big three", meaning they had the largest domains, and that they were the most powerful of the gods. After their father was defeated, the three brothers split up the realms that Saturn had once ruled -- the sky, the sea, and the underworld. Jupiter became the ruler of the sky, while Neptune became the ruler of the seas, and Pluto received dominion over the underworld. The key difference between the Roman god Pluto and his Greek counterpart Hades was the feelings of mortals toward these two versions of the same god. In Greece, Hades was considered evil, and was the most feared of the gods, while the Romans recognized all the good things that came from below the surface of the earth, such as precious metals and crops. Moreover the Romans did not fear death like the Greeks did; they believed in the possibility of a better life in the underworld. Pluto himself is usually depicted in all black, and with precious stones adorning his clothing. He is also often seen wearing his dark object, a helmet that was gifted to him by the Cyclops during the Titan War. Jupiter was given a master lightning bolt, Neptune received a trident, and Pluto was given the above-mentioned helmet, one which bestowed upon him the power of invisibility. As king of the underworld, his primary role was to judge dead mortals on their past lives, and then to dictate where they would be spending the rest of eternity -- in the Elysian Fields, in Tartarus, or in the Isles of the Blessed.

Nemesis
Engraving
Albrecht Dürer
1501

Nemesis was the god of revenge and retribution. She was most often mentioned in Greek tragedies, but like many other Greek gods, the Romans adopted her for their own ends. With all of the wars that the Roman empire waged, the goddess Nemesis was often worshipped, because of her function. She is often contrasted with the goddess Fortuna, and was considered a judge and jury for human actions. The most famous story regarding Nemesis was her involvement with the mortal Narcissus. Narcissus was a hunter and was known throughout the land to be very beautiful in his appearance. Because of his attributes, many people fell in love with him. However, he was very arrogant and rude to everyone, including his admirers. One day while he was hunting in the woods, a nymph by the name of Echo saw him and immediately fell in love with him. When she graciously and sweetly attempted her advances, Narcissus abruptly shoved her off of him and rejected him. Convinced that he was her one true love, Echo, roamed around in the forest in despair for the rest of her life, and died a sorrowful death. Nemesis, as the goddess of retribution, learned what had happened through the grapevine, and decided that Narcissus was in need of a wake-up call. The goddess found the hunter and led him to a small lake, where she used her power to get Narcissus to fall in love with his own reflection. The myth says that when Narcissus finally learned that the figure he had fallen in love with was his own reflection in the water, he committed suicide by throwing himself into that same lake, in a fit of despair. Nemesis is often depicted with wings and a sword; she also carries scales, which represent her dedication to righting wrongs, and seeking justice. The Romans respected such a figure, and dedicated a sanctuary to her in Rhamnous, an ancient Greek city in Attica. Because of this temple, Nemesis was also called Rhamnousia, as well as a separate given name, Invidia. Nemesis was also often mentioned in love stories, because of her connections with righteous behavior and the avenging of scorn. Toward this end, in some versions of the story of the Trojan War, Nemesis is said to have been the mother of Helen of Troy.

Venus

British Museum
London, England
1st or 2nd Century CE

The goddess Venus leaves her torso exposed as she stands straight. A mantle highlights her shoulders and drapes over her hips. This sculpture exhibits characteristics associated with the famous fourth-century BCE sculptor, Praxiteles. Workshops combined ancient Greek masterpieces with other styles to create new definitions of beauty. The goddess Venus is commonly known to be the Roman counterpart of the Greek goddess Aphrodite, goddess of love, beauty, and sexuality. However, like many of the other Roman gods and goddess, she had additional specialties and attributes than that of her Greek parallel; Venus is also perceived as the patron of fertility, prostitution, and victory. Married to the god Vulcan (god of fire), Venus is well renowned for her bitterness towards her husband, and flirtatious love towards the god of war, Mars. From all the myths, Venus was either lusted after or envied; by everyone, gods and men included. Anyone who looked upon her face, saw what they most desired, whether it was their ideal partner, or characteristics they wished they had. In both parallels, Venus and Aphrodite were considered to be major goddesses, or part of the "Big Twelve". However, they were not considered truly "powerful" because of their apparent uselessness in battle. What many failed to realize, however, was that the famous battles and tales still told today were often started by motives of love, lust, or jealousy. For example, it was said that the great Trojan War was indirectly caused by Venus, when she offered a Trojan shepherd named Paris the beautiful (and married) mortal Helen of Troy. Venus instigated Helen and Paris' relationship, which inevitably led to ten years of bloody conflict between the Trojans and the

Greeks. Many artistic works depicting Venus show her near the sea or standing naked on a clam shell. This portrayal is founded upon the idea that the goddess was born from the sea-foam, after Saturn cut up his father Uranus. His fallen remains fell down to earth from the heavens, and became the foam of the sea. Her origin story is unique, as all of the other gods were born from the next generation, making Venus the eldest Olympian. The goddess had many children, god and demi-god alike. Her most famous divine children were Phobos and Deimos, the gods of terror and panic, as well as Cupid, who was the god of match-making. Though Cupid has been modernized and commercialized, mythology recalls that the god was actually the divine counterpart of death, and that he was even more deadly than Death himself.

Caelestis
Capital Line Museum
Rome, Italy
3rd Century AD

Shown here are two sets of feet; this is not what one thinks about when imagining Roman mythology. These feet represent not a god or goddess, but an action -- the act of praying for good luck on an expedition. We are not exactly sure who Jovinus was, the person who made this offering, but they (Jovinus) made a vow to Caelestis, the patron goddess of safe voyages. Jovinus asked for safe passage on whatever journey they were making, and dedicated these stone footprints as an offering to the goddess. Caelestis was a goddess in various parts of the Mediterranean -- from Carthage in North Africa to Phoenicia in modern-day Israel and Lebanon. In fact, in Carthage, she was one of the main goddesses, and belief in her moved southward into the Sahara desert among the Berber people. She was married in Roman/Carthagenian belief to another god named Baal-Hamon. She appears to have had many names, such as Dea Caelestis, Juno Caelestis, or simply Caelestis. She was often identified as a moon goddess. Here, her intervention was being sought for the purpose of safe transit on a voyage (hence the appearance of stone feet, signifying travel of some sort). Since travelling was common in the far-flung Roman empire, it makes sense that people would have constantly needed to approach the gods for their help in moving from place to place. This surviving relic of that time (3rd century AD) shows us how common it was for people to seek this kind of help, as they went about their daily lives. She was known as Tanit in Rome at times, but was also absorbed into the cult of Aphrodite-Venus. Athletic games were sometimes held in her honor. Similar to this stone carving, Caelestis was thought to have been brought to Rome via a block of stone, and she blossomed in popularity during the 3rd century AD. She became known as the "mighty protectress of the Tarpeian Hill", showing her centrality to Roman beliefs in this later period.

Minerva as Warrior
Palazzo Massimo Museum
Rome, Italy
5th Century BCE (Augustan)

Arguably one of the most preserved statues in any classical statue collection, the goddess Minerva is presented here as a helmeted female warrior. Its large size leads experts to believe that this statue was used as a cult image, although many also think that it belonged in the temple of Minerva on the Aventine. Either way, this marble statue, dressed in a chiton and cloak covering the head, with an aegis plastered on her chest, can be identified as Minerva. Famous icons that are associated with Minerva include the fact that she is always wearing a chiton and a belt, and that she is always carrying around her shield, Aegis, which sports the head of Medusa on it. Aegis was feared and respected by all, and could part a crowd wherever Minerva walked. It was said that any mortal that looked upon the shield would immediately be turned to stone. This brings us to Minerva's history with the gorgon Medusa. Medusa was one of three gorgons, who was courting the sea-god Poseidon (Neptune, in Rome). One day Minerva caught Medusa and Neptune disrespecting one of Minerva's temples; they had been meeting there in secret to court one another, and Minerva was displeased. As punishment, Minerva transformed the previously beautiful mortal, Medusa, into a monstrous gorgon with a head full of snakes, which would turn any mortal that looked upon her into stone. Throughout mythology there have been many tales of Greek and Roman demi-gods alike who encountered Medusa. Since Minerva was also the goddess of handicrafts and arts in general, when a mortal named Arachne boasted that she was the best weaver, better than even Minerva herself, Minerva challenged her to a contest. When Arachne lost, Minerva changed her into a human-sized black-widow spider, as punishment for her boasting. It can be seen through mythology that both Medusa and Arachne tried to get revenge on Minerva in the forms of turning her children to stone, or having her children be born with a fear of spiders. Minerva today is still recognized as a synonym for wisdom. There are secret (and not so secret) societies in universities and other social institutions bearing the name, each with the connotation of creativity and intelligence or knowledge. Like many other deities, Minerva is often depicted with her sacred animal, the owl, which showed her acumen.

Minerva and Wisdom
Capital Line Museum
Rome, Italy
Second Half of the First Century AD (Flavian)

This bust is a copy of the image of Minerva which was part of the Capitoline Triad. This Triad includes sculptures of Minerva, Jupiter, and Juno, housed in the temple of Jupiter Optimus Maximus on Capitol Hill. Minerva is the Roman goddess of wisdom and strategic warfare, as well as arts, trade, and strategy. Known for her blonde hair, steel grey eyes, and horrifying shield, Aegis, Minerva is one of the major gods in Roman history. However, compared to her Greek counterpart, on whom the Romans first based her, Minerva was seen as a less aggressive form of Athena. The Romans thought of Minerva as less of a war goddess, and more of a goddess of wisdom, because they had their own set of war goddesses already (such as Bellona). Bellona was the Roman counterpart of the Greek Athena, who was seen as more warlike and martial than Minerva. The three goddesses Minerva, Diana, and Juno took a vow of chastity. In Greek mythology it was not uncommon for Athena to have demi-god children; they were said to be born the same way she had been in born (out of the skull of Zeus), so that she upheld her vows of chastity (but therefore she had children just the same). In Rome the fact that she had children was represented less commonly, so any children that she might have had with mortals were not seen as commanders in war or strategists, but as artists instead. Frankly, the Romans were appalled by the notion that Minerva could have children, simply because of the vows she took. They could not embrace how her children were claimed to have been born. However she was still respected by the Romans, and she was first worshipped in Rome along with Jupiter and Juno as part of the "capital line triad". Over the duration of the Roman Empire she became more and more important, and eventually she took over the Quinquatrus Festival, which launched the beginning of the campaign season for the Roman army. She became more important within the Roman army, and she became more associated with the concept of victory. This representation of Minerva would have been three meters high, but all that is left of the image is this bust.

Neptune
Coastal Roman Province
Sousse, Tunisia, North Africa
Mid-third century CE

In this image, a tile wall mosaic, Neptune can be seen riding his hippocampi, steeds who were half horses, and half fish. He is naked, as befits travel by sea, and a fish can be seen under the feet of one of the steeds. Neptune is the god of the sea, horses, and earthquakes. He is one of the three most important gods, the so-called Big Three, as he is the brother of Jupiter (Zeus) and Pluto (Hades). As Poseidon, his Greek counterpart, he is widely known as aggressive but playful. As Neptune, in his Roman form, he is more characteristically serious. This was not unusual, in that Roman gods tended to be more solemn than their Greek counterparts, because Roman culture had a greater respect for duty and devotion. Moreover, the Romans had a troubled relationship with the sea. Voyaging was dangerous, and had to be worked out with the gods through augurs and prophecies. Deemed the "mare nostrum", the Mediterranean Sea was Neptune's territory, so all disasters that happened at sea were blamed on Neptune, therefore losing prestige for the god among his Roman subjects when things went wrong. Taking Neptune's place by Jupiter's side was the god of war, Mars. His rivalry with Minerva was a famed motif in Roman mythology; it began when both Neptune and Minerva wanted to be patrons of the new city that would later be called Athens. When competing for the city, Neptune offered the people a water-fountain, while Minerva offered them an olive tree, both as presents. They left it to the local people who their patron would be. In the end, though the villagers were thankful for both gifts, they chose Minerva's olive tree, and dedicated the city to her name ("Athens"). Since that defeat,

Neptune and Minerva have existed in competition with each other. A trident is commonly associated with Neptune, and is seen in nearly all portrayals of the god. As his primary weapon, and symbol of power, the trident of Neptune was feared by all. First created by the three elder cyclops, it had great power over the sea, and could generate tsunamis, sea-foam, and earthquakes, all at once. Neptune had a great rivalry not only with Minerva, but also with his brother, the king of the Gods, Jupiter. As sons of Uranus, the evil Titan that ruled before the age of the gods, both deities craved power. Neptune, particularly jealous of Jupiter's status among the gods, tried to overthrow his brother many times.

Fortuna

J Paul Getty Museum
Los Angeles, California
1658

This painting is called "Allegory of Fortune", and it was rendered in 1658 by the painter Salvator Rosa. The image represents Fortuna, the goddess of luck and fortune, and she is holding the horn of plenty. Her Greek counterpart is the goddess of Tyche. Both goddesses were treated with more fear than love, but the Greeks were especially fearful as they believed Fortuna was the reason for many negative and unexpected events in life. For example, if a lazy or evil person was granted success or wealth in life without having to work for it, people assumed that the goddess had blessed them at birth, and was responsible. Tyche was most celebrated in Athens, as the locals there believed she favored their city, while Fortuna was worshipped the most in ancient Italy. Both goddesses were usually depicted holding the horn of plenty, or the cornucopia, as the item represented their power in assuring abundance. Moreover, a common portrayal of Tyche was of her standing on a rolling ball, which represented uncertainty and the precariousness of chance. The Romans, in keeping with their stereotypes, were more respectful to the goddess, and believed that she was able to bless mankind. The goddess was worshipped the most before wartime, and was more important to the Romans than to the Greeks, overall. Her counterpart was the goddess Nemesis, who was the being in charge of revenge and retribution. Tyche was the figurehead of many Greek coins during the Hellenistic period, and Fortuna was also well-represented in Roman coins. The Greeks depicted Tyche in two personalities; as Tyche, she represented more of the downsides of her patronage, such as uncertainty and bad fortune. Her other personality as

Eutychia, portrayed her in a more favorable light, emphasizing her ability to give out good fortune, prosperity, and all manner of positive things. These two personalities were very distinct, and could be easily distinguished in artworks from the period. Tyche would hold a rudder in her hand, representing her ability to influence the course of events, and would also be seen standing on a ball, as above. Eutychia was sometimes pictured with wings or a crown, which symbolized the better parts of the goddesses' personality and powers.

Sol
Capital Line Museum
Rome, Italy
Second Half of 1st Century AD

First known as Sol Indiges, this god was one of the first gods of Roman mythology. He was first introduced to the world by Emperor Titus of the Flavian dynasty. After disappearing from history for a brief amount of time, the god was reintroduced as Sol Invictus by Emperor Aurelian in 274 AD. During this time, Sol Invictus was worshipped as a prime god in Rome, up until Christianity took over as the main religion during Constantine's rule (300s AD). However, Christianity and astrology and the sun have always been deeply connected. An example of this can be seen in the connection between Christmas day and the pagan holiday celebration of Sol Invictus, both on December 25. Though Apollo is usually associated with being the sun god, because he was such a major god and patron of so many other things, there were other gods such as Sol who had a more primary relation to the sun. One of these other gods was the Greek sun god Helios, who was said to be one of the first gods, but whose powers and identity were taken over by Apollo. Before Christianity, the worship of the god Sol in his many forms was primarily through sun cults. Moreover, many Roman emperors such as Elagabalus and Aurelian built many temples to commemorate and worship Sol. Thus, Sol took on the role as patron and protector of Roman emperors. Sol's two names, Sol Indiges and Sol Invictus (the latter of which means "Unconquered Sun"), were to help separate the two timelines and myths of this god. Sol Indiges was introduced during a time when the Trojan hero Aeneas took refuge in Italy after the fall of Troy. There he married the daughter of a Latin king. This king was the son of Circe, a sorceress and daughter of the sun god. Aeneus' marriage to the great-granddaughter of Sol represented his influence and importance in the Roman state. We know less about Sol Invictus, but given that his birthday is on December 25th, it is said that Western churches in later centuries established Advent, the pre-season for Christmas. Finally, it's interesting to note that Sol Invictus was the figurehead on many ancient Roman coins, given that many emperors of that era preferred to worship this god, including Constantine the Great, who steered Rome toward Christianity.

Ulysses
Palazzo Massimo Museum
Rome, Italy
1st Century BCE

Odysseus's Roman name was Ulysses. Among one of the few well preserved wall paintings of the first century BCE, this fresco depicts a scene from the famous story "the Odyssey" in which Ulysses, the main protagonist and Greek hero of the story, is tied up to the mast of his ship and stuffs his ear with beeswax as he passes the sirens. These creatures would use their sweet voices and powerful magic to lure sailors and explorers to their lair where the monsters would eat them. They had beautiful voices, and could transform themselves to look like anyone that passing sailors wanted to see. But in reality, they were hideous, scaly monsters, horrible to look at in every way. Ulysses was king of the island of Ithaca, and is one of the most famous Greek heroes in mythology whose stories have been transmitted to today. Many stories were written about him, most famously that of his adventures in trying to return home to Ithaca after the Trojan War. However, his most famous role in the Trojan War was in the episode concerning the Trojan horse. The Trojan horse was a trick devised by the Greeks to attempt to infiltrate the city of Troy. What appeared as a huge wooden gift was actually a hollow horse filled with Greek soldiers, including Ulysses himself. The Greek soldiers waited inside the belly of the horse until nightfall, after all of the Trojans had celebrated and drank themselves into a stupor. At that point, the soldiers quietly exited the sculpture, and proceeded to kill as many Trojans as possible, and destroyed the city itself. This happened because the Greeks had been trying to get into the walls of Troy for years, but had been unsuccessful. With this, the conclusion of the Trojan War, Ulysses spent ten years trying to return to his home of Ithaca. On his voyage home, he encountered many famous monsters and trials. These included the sirens mentioned above in this artwork, but also the Lotus-Eaters, where Ulysses was held captive with his men through the consumption of sleep-inducing lotuses. Another trial was the famous encounter with the giant cyclops Polyphemus, whom he escaped by introducing himself as "nobody". A third adventure was with the sorcerer Circe, who turned many of his men into pigs, but who eventually became infatuated with Ulysses, and let him go. Scylla and Charibdis were two monsters on both sides of a maritime strait, equally horrible, and Ulysses escaped them both (though many of his men were killed in the process). Finally, Ulysses spent seven years on the island of Ogygia with the witch Calypso, who held him captive through her curse.

Saturn

Cigarette Card (16th of 25 Cards In Collection)
Boguslavsky "Mythological Gods and Goddesses"
1942

Saturn, like his Greek counterpart Kronos, was often considered an antagonist in ancient mythologies. However, the Romans later adopted him and reinvented him into being a god of the harvest.. Though at times he was considered a god, he was actually the king of the Titans, a class of beings who ruled the earth before the gods came to be. In ancient mythology, the Titans were told to be children of Uranus and Gaea, the sky and earth deities. Saturn had always been the leader of his siblings, and strived to rule the universe. When they all became old enough, Saturn overthrew his father, Uranus, and became the celestial king. He is the Titan of time, and was said to have the power to slow it down, especially during battles, so that he could vanquish his enemies before they even realized that he was advancing. As described previously, different stories recount different events, but one of the most famous tales that involved Saturn was how he ate his own children. He only ruled during the epoch of what was considered to be the golden age of the ancient world. That story is told in more detail under Jupiter's rubric, but suffice to say here that Saturn ended up vomiting up his children after his wife poisoned him. After this story, the gods took over and Saturn was dethroned and cut to pieces by his own scythe, the symbol of his power and his chosen weapon. Some myths say that a younger group of Titans killed him; other myths say that the gods (the ones he had vomited up) were the ones who committed this deed. However, many myths agree that the remains of Saturn were thrown into the deepest realms of Tarturus, the Hell dimension of the underworld. Romans believed that Saturn was a complex deity and that he should be given the chance to atone for his sins. As such, after becoming a god of the harvest, many Romans sacrificed to him, and included him in their daily prayers and worship. He even inspired a famous festival that all Romans looked forward to, called Saturnalia. It was originally celebrated on December 17th annually, and the day was used for freeing the populace from Rome's strict social and class-based rules. Festivities included banquets, drinking, gladiatorial games, etc, but also people wearing casual clothes, and masters and slaves reversing their roles.

Aglibol and Malakbel
Capital Line Museum
Rome, Italy
235-236 AD

Caios Aurelios Heliodoros Adrianos donated this relief to the gods of the fatherland, Aglibol and Malakbel, at his own expense in order to save himself, his wife, and his children. Aglibol originated from an immigrant community in what is today known as Syria. As god of the moon, Aglibol had a sibling and companion, Malakbel, the god of the sun. Similarities can be drawn here between Aglibol and Malakbel and the traditional Roman twins, Diana and Apollo. Moreover, Aglibol was part of a divine triad, along with the gods Bel and Yarhibol. However, this triad was not a group of individuals possessing equal powers. Most if not all depictions of Aglibol and Malakbel show the lunar god at the right, representing his supposed superiority to the sun god (on the left). Aglibol and Malakbel were gods of long-standing in the Middle East; they pre-dated the Roman Empire, so it is interesting to see them as still being important and represented in Roman times. This triad showed the fusion of Parthian, Hellenistic and Roman belief systems meeting and mixing in sculptural form. Malakbel's name was derived from Babylonion origin, and was primarily worshipped by the ancient Syrian city of Palmyra. Moreover, Malakbel was often identified by the Romans with their sun god, Sol, and by the Greeks and their gods, Zeus and Hermes. Greeks identified Malakbel with Hermes as he was also known to be a messenger god, as was Hermes. Another connection was made between the god Malakbel and the Babylonian sun god Shamash. With Malakbel we see that many cultures and peoples had their own versions of the same god, in this case a sun god (the Greeks had Apollo, the Romans Sol, the Babylonians Shamash, etc.). Naturally, the god of the sun was often portrayed with his sibling, the god of the moon. Aglibol is most commonly associated with the cult of Bel (of whom he was in a divine triad with). Those within the cult are known to act as Aglibol's attendants. Often portrayed in military dress and a halo around his head, Aglibol was represented as the stereotypical god of the moon. These two siblings were also associated with other Syrian deities, such as Astarte and Arsu, the goddesses of heaven and the god of camels. Aglibol and Malakbel are most famous for being venerated alongside each other in the "Sacred Wood" sanctuary.

Terminus
Cleveland Museum of Art
Cleveland, OH
1532

During the Italian Renaissance, Erasmus of Rotterdam (active from roughly 1466-1536), the renowned Dutch scholar and humanist, took in Greek and Roman culture and infused many of its ethical and philosophical meanings into his own work. The lowland painter Holbein here conflates Erasmus's image with that of Terminus, the god of boundaries in Rome, who defied Jupiter by keeping his own position atop Capitoline Hill. Erasmus adopted this grit and determination of Terminus, along with the saying "concedo nulli" ("I give in to no one"), as a symbol for his own resolve and devotion. Terminus himself was the god of boundaries and borders. He was first created after the Roman state decreed that everyone should mark the boundaries of their property with stone. The placement of these stones was seen to be sacred, and therefore they had to be installed through a religious ceremony or sacrifice, led by priests. These sacrifices were usually of food, as it was unlawful to stain boundary stones with the blood of living animals. These became sacred boundaries and were not only relevant in private homes, but in state boundaries as well. It was common decency for foreign peoples not to cross over these boundaries, for doing so would potentially be seen as an act of war. Many statues of the Roman god were built within the empire, especially in front of wealthy patrons' estates, and in front of royal or religious properties. The most famous Terminus statue actually resided in the most well-known temple of Jupiter in the Capitol. Moreover, as the patron of boundaries and security, the statue could never be covered by a roof or any other material. The marble above the statue within the temple of Jupiter was destroyed, in order to maintain that tradition. The name Terminus in Latin in fact means "marker". One of the most important aspects of Terminus was his association with the king of the gods himself, Jupiter. Not only did their depictions look alike, temples of Jupiter were usually built upon the temples of lesser gods, sometimes those of Terminus himself, and statues of Terminus were likewise in temples of Jupiter. In this form, Terminus was occasionally identified as "Jupiter Terminalis", a mixture of the two gods.

Salus

Herzog Anton Ulrich Museum
Braunschweig, Germany
1589

Salus was the Roman goddess of safety and welfare. She was the daughter of Asclepius, the figure/god of medicine, making her the granddaughter of Apollo. She is often depicted with a snake or various grains as a symbol of prosperity. With such an important function in the ancient world, it is not a surprise that priests would often pray to her and make her offering, in exchange for the safety and well-being of not just Rome itself, but its inhabitants, including animals. On August 5th, a festival with circus games and the public spectacle of the sacrificing of a cow was made in her honor. Though she is considered a minor goddess, she has many temples in Italy, including one on Quirinal Hill, which was erected in 302 BCE. Interestingly enough, that same temple was hit by lightning not once but twice, in 276 BCE and 206 BCE, respectively. Not only was it partly destroyed by the electric current of the lightning, there was also a fire in the first century CE that damaged the temple. Nevertheless, the temple still stood after many restorations until the fourth century CE. She appeared on Roman coins largely until the reign of emperor Constantine I. She was known by many titles, including Salus Publica, Salus Augusti, and most famously Salus Romana. Ovid, the famous Roman poet, even mentions her in his poems, and states that an offering should be made to her along with Janus and Pax on March 30th of every year. Salus was also associated with salt (salt in Latin was "sal", which made up part of her name). Romans had already figured out that salt had antiseptic effects, and salt was further connected to the goddess because of its connection to health and hygiene. Many if not all traditional household shrines contained a small collection of salt, known then as salinum, which was a key component of ancient Roman rituals. For example, salt was often mixed with flour, and was scattered on the heads of animals that were to be sacrificed. This ritual signified the purity of both the animals and the practice itself. Salis was also associated with healing waters, holy waters and cleansing baths. The modern-day word "spa" is thought to be an acronym derived from a Latin saying "Salus per aquam", which meant "health through water". Salus' importance in everyday Roman life was especially evident in this area, with the prevalence of public bath-houses, which were not only a place for physical cleansing, but also of spiritual and religious rejuvenation.

Polyphemus as Lover
Palazzo Massimo Museum
Rome, Italy
1st century AD

Used for decorative purposes, this relief depicts the myth of the cyclops Polyphemus, identifiable by the singular eye on his forehead, and his unrequited love for the personification of sea foam, the nymph Galatea. Polyphemus is shown here as a shepherd with a syrinx, which is a musical instrument, and a crown of wheat adorning his head. We have already seen that he possessed many sheep, and these animals always are shown in portrayals of the giant. Mythological accounts recall that Polyphemus loved the nereid Galatea, a water-nymph, but she loved another. When Polyphemus discovered Galatea and her lover, the cyclops killed her lover by crushing him with a boulder. Galatea transformed the blood of her lover, Acis, into a river that was located at the bottom of Mount Aetna, one of Europe's most active volcanoes. The river was named after Acis. These types of stories seem to happen a lot in Roman mythology. Unrequited tales of love often lead to the death of one of the lovers, and the naming of a river or a mountain is common as a testament to the story. Other accounts in mythology depict Galatea as accepting Polyphemus' courtship, but it was universally understood that she did not actually love him. She did however enjoy the attention of such a famous personage. Polyphemus has one eye, but has the facial shape of a human, meaning that he had eye sockets on either side of his great, central eye. These sockets however were empty. Depictions of Polyphemus because of this were often very frightening, and because of his tendency to eat heroes, like some of Odysseus' men. In general, gods don't love their children in the modern sense of the term, but this story shows that Neptune looked after his son. Polyphemus' location on the island of Sicily was one of a number of stories that took place on this island. The legend of Scylla and Charybdis also took place there, for example. Sicily was something of an outlying area to the Roman Empire, which was more concerned with the boot of Italy. The Romans placed their monsters at some distance to themselves, showing a distrust of the frontier and places they did not know as well as their own home soil. This is why mythological demi-god quests were so selective and feared, but also honorable, because only a real hero could survive the threats and monsters of such places.

Polyphemus as Monster
Capital Line Museum
Rome, Italy
2nd Century BC

Polyphemus is a famous cyclops in Greek and Roman mythology, featured in the Odyssey. In the renowned poem written by Homer, the protagonist, Odysseus, is trapped by Polyphemus in his cave. As a herder, Polyphemus owned a lot of sheep, which Odysseus would later use to his advantage during a timely escape. Polyphemus himself was a giant, and was a son of Neptune, the god of the sea. He inhabited the island of Sicily, which became known as the island of the Cyclops in mythology. Odysseus and his men, while on a quest to try to return to their homeland of Ithaca, encountered the giant after wandering into a cave. They were trying to capture and hopefully eat some of Polyphemus' sheep. Once they were all inside the cave, however, Polyphemus appeared, rolled a boulder over the entrance, and trapped them inside. The giant then consumed several of Odysseus' men, terrifying the others who were in fear for their lives. Odysseus, quick on his feet, offered Polyphemus a strong wine, which got the giant drunk. When Polyphemus asked for Odysseus' name, the hero replied that his name was "No one". Odysseus blinded the giant while he was in his intoxicated sleep. Given that Polyphemus was a Cyclops, with only one eye, he was permanently blinded and could not see Odysseus or his men. Polyphemus awoke and started yelling for help from his brethren, but when the other giants arrived, Polyphemus could only tell him that "No one" had done this to him. Odysseus and his men escaped on the under-bellies of his sheep, while Polyphemus felt the top parts of each sheep's back, trying to find them in his blinded state. Having reached his boat, Odysseus turned around and taunted Polyphemus by revealing his true name. However, his ego was his downfall, as Polyphemus prayed to his father, Neptune, to punish him and his crew. Neptune caused Odysseus' ship to further deviate from their normal route home. It ended up taking Odysseus ten years to return to Ithaca. The moral of this story was not to be boastful, especially with the son of a god. On this side of the large vase shown, the krater depicts the blinding of Polyphemus by Odysseus in his attempt to escape the cyclops' cave. The Romans loved this story as a cautionary tale.

Vulcan
Endcliffe Hall
Sheffield, UK
1855-1866

This is a statue of Vulcan from England. The carving is by the stone-smiths Mawer and Ingle, at Endcliffe Hall, Sheffield, in South Yorkshire, England. It was designed by Sir John Brown (1816-1896), and built between the years 1863-1865. The sculpture shows Hephaestus (the Roman Vulcan), god of fire, metal-working and crafts, from a panel at the base of the west tower. Vulcan was the son of the king of the gods, Jupiter, and his wife Juno. With such important and divine parents, everyone expected him to be extremely handsome, but when he was born, he was horrifyingly ugly. His mother, Juno, was so disgusted with him, that she threw him off the top of Mount Olympus as a child. When he finally hit the water of earth below, he broke one of his legs and it never healed properly, giving him a noticeable limp for the rest of his (immortal) life. Growing up, he was constantly ridiculed and shamed for his appearance, especially his walk, due to his broken leg and the fall. Most ashamed of him at all was his mother, but one day Vulcan discovered metalwork and fire, and he learned and perfected this craft over time. He was able to make the most beautiful jewelry and the most deadly weapons, and though still horrified by his appearance, Juno asked her son for a hand-crafted throne, which would rival any other made in history. Vulcan decided to get revenge on his mother for the way she treated him by ensnaring the queen of the gods in her new throne. Juno of course was unaware of this plot, as the chair he made for her was so beautiful, constructed with gold, silver, and pearls. However, when she went to sit in it, her weight triggered hidden springs and metal harnesses that strapped the goddess to the chair.

She was stuck in the chair for days as no one had the skull that Vulcan possessed to release her from the contraption. Finally, her husband Jupiter proposed a compromise. If Vulcan would release his mother from the chair, Jupiter would grant Vulcan the most beautiful immortal to be his wife, the goddess of love and beauty, Venus. Vulcan was also famous in mythology for having fashioned Pandora's box, mankind's punishment for retaining the secret of fire. The box, when opened, released disease, old age, evil and war, all of the things that would curse mankind for ages. All in exchange for fire.

Vesta
Silver Denarius of P Sulpicius Galba
Found in Nottinghamshire, UK
Used in 69 BCE

Vesta was the virgin goddess of the hearth, home, and family in Roman mythology. Her dominion represented community and camaraderie, which was very important to the Romans. She is usually depicted stoking and maintaining a fire, which was her primary role in Olympus, up in the clouds. As the eldest child of Saturn and Rhea, she was the first to be swallowed by her father. But paradoxically, she is often considered the youngest, because she was the last child to be regurgitated. The goddess took a vow of celibacy, and is associated with virginity and innocence, so she usually appears as a young girl, fully clothed in white garments. Common symbols of the goddess were the donkey and the kettle. The donkey represented her patronage of baking, as the fire she stoked was crucial to the making of bread. The donkey's role as the strong, millstone-turner resonated with her character. The kettle represented the Romans' need for her fire and hearth for their everyday uses. In ancient Rome, the only female priests, called the Vestal Virgins, tended to the central fire that burned in the sacred temple of Vesta. The Romans believed that the extinguishing of this fire would bring bad omens to the empire, so the protection and tending of this fire was important. These special priestesses were selectively chosen and taken for their homes, brought to the sacred temple all under the age of ten. For thirty years they would take a vow of chastity and spend their time studying religious rituals, and tending the fire. Another ten years were spent teaching the next generation of vestal virgins. Although most former vestal virgins chose not to marry, it was considered an honor to marry one. After they were relieved of their duty, the old priestesses were indeed allowed to marry, usually arranged by the pontus maximus, a high priest who was the supervisor of all of the virgins. Each year on March 1st there was a ceremony to renew the sacred fire. Vesta also had her own festival called Vestalia, which was unique in that it was celebrated only by women. The festival comprised a procession of barefoot women to the temple of Vesta in the Roman Forum, where the sacred fire was burning. Though she is now commonly overlooked as a central goddess, she was a key part of every Roman household, as the hearth was central to the kitchen, the home, and therefore, to the family.

Ceres
Aberdeen's Union Chambers, formerly Clydesdale Bank
Aberdeen, Scotland
Rebuilt in 1840

This statue of Ceres, on top of Aberdeen's Union Chambers, shows the goddess of agriculture and the harvest sitting atop a building in Scotland. Ceres was an especially important goddess due to her patronage over general food production (such as grain) during Roman times. The goddess (whose Greek counterpart is Demeter) is usually depicted in a flowing chiton, holding a woven basket of colorful fruits, and she is adorned with various flowers. The origin story of Ceres is one of the oldest and most well-known stories in mythology. The evil titan and father of the gods, Saturn, was given a prophecy warning of his demise at the hands of one of his unborn children. When Rhea, Saturn's wife and the mother of the gods, gave birth to six divine children, Saturn swallowed five of his children whole, fearful of being overthrown by any one of them. Little did he know, Rhea had secretly hidden the sixth child, Jupiter, and had given her husband a giant rock to swallow instead. Even the divine can't digest boulders, so Saturn vomited up his five children, Ceres being one of them. In the end, Saturn was overthrown by his children, just as the prophecy had predicted. These children, led by Jupiter, the one who had been hidden by his mother, were Neptune, Pluto, Juno, Vesta (and Ceres). The most famous story of Ceres actually centers around her only daughter Proserpina (or Persephone in the Greek legends). Proserpina was kidnapped by the god of the underworld, Pluto, and was dragged down to the land of the dead. She fought and screamed but by the time her mother Ceres had arrived, there was no longer any trace of her. It is said that Ceres traveled the earth for nine days in search of her daughter, and called upon mortals to help in her quest. By the tenth day, the god of the sun, Apollo, who had witnessed the kidnapping, finally came clean and told Ceres what had happened. By the time Ceres made it down to the underworld and confronted Pluto, he had already tricked Proserpina into wearing a magic pomegranate that bound her to Pluto and the underworld. Ceres was furious and traveled back up to Olympus to act for Jupiter's help. The situation escalated, but eventually a compromise was reached: Proserpina would spend half of the mortal year in the underworld, and the other half with her mother on earth. It is said that this agreement is the reason we have the seasons that we do. Spring and summer reflect Ceres' mood of happiness, when her daughter is on earth. Fall and Winter, the colder half of the year, is when she is with her husband Pluto.

Bacchus

Palazzo Massimo Museum
Rome, Italy
1080

This mosaic features the god Bacchus, in which his grapevine wreath and leopard skin toga are immediately distinguishable. The equivalent of the Greek god Dionysus, Bacchus was infamous for being the god of wine. However, few know that both forms of the god were patrons of many other things, including agriculture, fertility, drama, and revelry. The two aspects of the god were also said to be quite intense as Dionysus was known to be a loud, drunken partier while Bacchus was quieter, and more strict -- in other words, much more Roman. Bacchus was unique among the big twelve" (major Gods) as he was originally a demi-god, a son of Jupiter and a mortal named Semele. After his many quests and displays of heroism as a mortal, the gods granted him divine status, and he was eventually promoted to one of the twelve seers of Jupiter's council. Given that Jupiter was already married to the goddess Juno, when Juno learned about her husband's affair, she set out with a plan to punish Semele, knowing she could not punish her husband. Understanding that mortals could not see a god or goddess in their true, divine form, Juno tricked Semele into seeing Jupiter in just such a guise. Because she was a mortal, Semele basically spontaneously combusted upon viewing her divine lover, and was destroyed. Bacchus himself is often portrayed as a bearded, middle-aged man, with a wreath of grapevines adorning his head. Additionally, he is often seen carrying a thyrsus, a staff with a pinecone attached to the head of it (a symbol of his power). As the god of agriculture and wine, he was always followed by a procession of mortals who celebrated and adored him. A considerable reason for this was that he could turn water into wine, which (other than the fact that it was alcohol), awed his followers into believing he was God himself. Bacchus was integrated into Roman state religion in the third century B.C.E. by the mysterious cult of Dionysus. This cult re-introduced Bacchus as a combination of the Greek god Dionysus and the Italian wine-god Liber. The god Liber was part of a trio worshipped by poor, lower-class Romans called the Aventine triad. The most important festival in Rome featuring the god was called Bacchanalia. The festival obviously boasted a lot of drinking and merriment, and was usually held in the countryside and at vineyards. This was partly because Bacchus believed that cities were too unnatural and boring. This word (bacchanalia) is still used in English today to signify a really good party.

Folk Understandings and Prayers
Palazzo Massimo Museum
Rome, Italy
37-41 CE (Caligula)

These bronze arms were part of a decorative ensemble with the purpose of warding off evil. Originally, they were on the front of a Roman ship, and they had the use of keeping misfortune at bay. It was not only the case that Romans prayed to recognizable gods from their pantheon. There was an everyday sort of belief system, too, that allowed common people to pray for common things (like the safety of a seaborne voyage across dangerous waters). Having arms outstretched in front of a ship clearly was this sort of belief. What's being invoked here is not the particular help of any major (or minor) god, but more the idea of general help from the various spirits that inhabited the world. This is important because it shows the kind of everyday beliefs that everyday people had, not the higher beliefs in gods or goddesses whom we all recognize now as part of the Roman spiritual pantheon. Although Roman gods and goddesses penetrated into the population, the functions of these gods and their histories tended to be more complex among the elite classes. But it was working-class Romans who took ships, and went on everyday journeys on the sea. These were the people that needed spiritual guidance and protection, even if they did not own the boats. It is interesting to compare and contrast their needs with those of the elite Roman class. We can compare this to the version of Christianity or Judaism practiced right now, in places like the Vatican (for Christians) or in Jerusalem (for Jews). Everyday Christians and Jews may not have the same day-to-day concerns with spirituality that the more elite members of their religions possess. In this case, the outstretched arms tell a story of immediate needs, not a more abstract connection to the world of the gods. Social stratification affected the mindset of religion, day to day. A dependence on religion is often necessary because people need something to turn to in times of stress. Commoners needed to have "invisible hands" guiding them, and to be able to hold an idea accountable, when they could not hold elites or leaders accountable themselves. Thus these outstretched hands represent the common man's religion, in many ways: a plea for guidance or help toward earthly demands that were believed to be acquired from common spirits, not the high celestial world of the gods.

Iris

New York Public Library
New York City, USA
1875

Iris is the goddess of the rainbow, as well as the messenger of the gods. She is usually depicted as a young woman, with wings and carrying a water pitcher. This pitcher was meant to symbolize her ability to make a rainbow anywhere she went, the water being a key ingredient in this construction. Some myths reported that she used this pitcher to carry water from the river Styx which was a river in the underworld that separated the living and the dead. As such Iris was considered an important bridge between the mortal and the divine realm. She was considered to be the female equivalent of Mercury, the primary god of travel and messages between divine beings. Though some tales recount that she was unmarried, others say that she fell in love with Zephyros, the god of the west wind. In these stories it is said that Iris and Zephyros had a son named Pothos, a minor god of desire. As a messenger to the gods, Iris was a permanent character in Mount Olympus, and used her pitcher at times to serve nectar to the gods, the preferred drink of the divine. When a god needed a message delivered to another god or mortal, they would go to Iris because she was able to travel very fast between Olympus and earth, and could even journey into the underworld, a place that most of the other gods avoided. Another method of message transportation was via one of her rainbows, where someone could throw a golden drachma into a body of water, chant Iris' name, and be able to have a holographic "video conference" with anyone of their choosing. Iris was also said to be associated with Juno, the queen of the gods, as a servant to her. Her parentage is uncertain, though she was known to be the sister of the famous Harpies, who were half-bird and half-human, and hideous in all ways. On the contrary, Iris was considered to be one of the most beautiful goddesses, alongside Venus, the goddess of love and beauty herself. Her name is derived from the Greek word for rainbow, Iris, and can still be seen in the modern English word iridescent, meaning "giving off color and beauty". Iris is frequently mentioned in Homer's Iliad, where she is seen scolding the gods for interfering in the Trojan War, transmitting communications between Helen of Troy and her confidantes, and even encouraging Achilles to rescue the dead body of his friend from a battlefield.

Proserpina
Eurydice's Tomb
Vergina, Greece
340 BCE

Proserpina was the goddess of agriculture. She was also the daughter of Jupiter and the wife of Pluto, the king of the underworld. Her mother was Ceres, the goddess of Spring. The most famous tale regarding Proserpina was how she was abducted by Pluto, and brought to the underworld where she was forced to marry and live with him. Her mother, Jupiter, and many other beings searched for weeks before they found her, but they were too late. The innocent Proserpina had already been tricked into eating one of the underworld's pomegranates, which meant that she would forever be bound to that dimension. Ceres and Jupiter made an agreement with Pluto stating that Prosperpina would stay in the underworld with him for a third of the year, but would return to the mortal realm for the other two thirds of the year. This story was told to account for the changes in the seasons. When Proserpina was with Pluto, that represented the winter months; this was when her mother Ceres was grief-stricken, and dormant. However when she was in her mother's company, Ceres was happy, and granted the earth warmer weather and more sunlight. This particular story was a very popular inspiration for art throughout history, with artworks dating all the way back to at least 340 BCE, like the one shown here, though possibly much earlier. There have even been frescoes and mosaics found in royal tombs which carry her likeness, and the story of her life. The very dramatic story of her abduction found its way into many Roman sarcophagi, and continued to be used by many eighteenth and nineteenth century artists. Similar to many other Roman deities, there were various cults that especially worshipped Proserpina.

Such cults were particularly present in Sicily and southern Italy. Many annual festivities were also celebrated in her honor, for example the Thesmophoria, which was an exclusively female festival that celebrated both Proserpina and Ceres, her mother. This particular event was held right before Spring, which was the start of the sowing period for agriculture. A particularly interesting aspect of Thesmophoria was the mixing of pickled pig remains with the seeds that were to be sown into the ground. The pig remains were sustenance for the seeds, and were thought to make the ground more fertile.

Mars as Soldier
Museo Nacional del Prado
Madrid, Spain
1640

Mars is the god of war; his name was Ares in Ancient Greece. He was the most important and prominent military god among Roman deities, second only to Jupiter in the entire Roman pantheon. He is the son of Jupiter and Juno. In mythology he is described as having hollow eyes with fires in them. Like many other gods, he is calmer and more obedient in his Roman aspect than in his Greek manifestations. In Greek mythology he is known to start fights for fun, and to love violence and conflict and blood; as a Roman, he presented duty and leadership instead. He was the father of Romulus and Remus, the twin brothers who founded the city of Rome. Because of this connection to the origins of Rome itself, Mars had real importance and respect. His symbols included a wolf (the animals that suckled Romulus and Remus), and the color red (for blood). He was always seen as a protector of the Roman army, and while he was revered by humans, Mars was still unpopular among the gods because of his personality. He was said to be difficult, and he argued a lot; he was always seeking more power for himself. Phobos and Deimos, another set of sons of Mars and Venus (the goddess of love, his consort) were minor gods who represented panic and terror, respectively They often accompanied Mars in battle to spread fear amongst his enemies. The Romans had festivals in Mars' honor, the biggest of which was celebrated in March, the month named after the god himself. On this day people celebrated the new year, on the first day of March, which was said to be when Mars was first born. Festivities included dancing, fairs, and animal sacrifices. The festivals that celebrated Mars often coincided with military campaign seasons, thus being celebrated from March to October. Mars was also part of an ancient triad of gods (the Archaic Triad) which included Jupiter, a god named Quirinus, and himself. The priests of this sect were called the Salii, who prayed to and celebrated these three in ceremonies of song, while dressed in bronze armor. Mars was one of the most important of the gods, especially in his Roman form, as shown by his frequent appearances.

Mars as Paramour
Perigord Art and Archeology Museum
Périgueux, France
1824

This image, by the great French painter David, shows Mars being disarmed by the Graces. Mars was known as a womanizer, and though he was very powerful and someone to be feared, he had a difficult time resisting their charms. He even sought the goddess Minerva who was known for being virginal and for spurning romantic advances. Most notably his courtship with the goddess of love, Venus, was shown in many artistic representations from Antiquity to the present. A famous story tells of Vulcan, Venus' husband, catching Mars and Venus in his bed. Though enraged, Vulcan bided his time, and crafted (being the god of fire and metallurgy) an invisible net, that he laid on his marriage bed. When Mars and Venus were on the bed subsequently, the net immediately ensnared them, while Vulcan gathered all of the other gods to watch and mock the couple. Mars never lived down this incident and deeply resented Vulcan for this public humiliation. Mars is commonly depicted as having a helmet and spear, as well as full armor with a red cape marking his divinity as the patron of war and bloodshed. The spear was to Mars what the lightning bolt was to Zeus; it was his symbol, and his chosen weapon. Gods and humans alike feared his javelin, and what he could do with it. Humans sacrificed various animals to this god on certain occasions. Most common was the sacrifice of rams and bulls, and on special occasions he was offered a triple offering of a pig, a ram, and a bull, an uncommon honor. Moreover, he was the only known god to receive offerings of a horse (horses were usually seen as too important and special to sacrifice; this further showed Mars' honor and respect within the Roman ranks).

Though his Greek form was characterized more by a tendency to enjoy and incite war, the Romans viewed him as a means toward peace through war, not as a harbinger of death and destruction (as Ares was in Greece). Some Roman emperors re-named themselves after the god, to suggest their supposed divinity, and the power given to them by Mars himself.

Medusa
Palazzo Massimo Museum
Rome, Italy
2nd Century CE

Made during the mid-second century, this mosaic depicts a familiar tale of the hero Perseus decapitating the gorgon with the help of Minerva. The gorgon Medusa is shown here on a large black and white mosaic shield. Portrayed with snakes for hair, the mosaic features a beautiful border along with four angular decorations. Garnishing the edges are mosaic plants and birds eating cherries. Medusa was one of three Gorgon sisters born from the monsters Phorcys and Ceto. Medusa, the most famous of the three, had snakes for hair. Her special power was that any mortal who looked directly at her would be turned to stone. In earlier fables, Medusa and her two sisters were born monsters, but in later myths, Medusa was the only one with hair comprised of snakes, and the power to turn people to stone. This power was supposedly a punishment from the goddess Minerva for having sexual interactions with the god Neptune in Minerva's temple. However Minerva later used this to her advantage when she adopted Medusa's hideous appearance to be on her shield, Aegis, so that her enemies would cower in fear. The most famous example of this is on the gigantic statue of the Athena parthenos, in which Medusa's head is carved onto the goddess's breast-plate. As such, many Roman warriors adopted this design and carved a Gorgon's head onto their shields or armor. This symbol of warding off evil was also used as bronze end-pieces on Roman ships. The most famous story regarding Medusa was the tale of her death at the hands of the demigod Perseus. After Minerva turned Medusa into a hideous monster, Perseus was sent on a quest by the gods to find and behead this monster. In this account, he received help in the form of artifacts from four different gods: Pluto, who gave Perseus a cap of invisibility; Mercury, who gave Perseus a pair of his famous winged sandals; Minerva, who gave him an impenetrable bronze shield, and finally Vulcan, who forged him a sword. Using his gifts, Perseus tracked Medusa to a cave where he found her asleep. Using his shield, so as to not look at her directly and thus be turned to stone, the hero was able to creep up on the monster and behead her. From her neck, the dying Medusa birthed two children: Pegasus, the winged horse, and Chrysaor, a demigod who would later become a famed pirate. Both children were born from the Gorgon and the god Neptune. Perseus wrapped up Medusa's head and used it for other quests to turn his enemies into stone.

Somnus
Galleria Borghese
Rome, Italy
1774

Somnus was the Roman name for the Greek god Hypnos, the personified spirit of sleep. He was one of the many children of the goddess of night, Nyx, and the god of darkness, Erebus. Somnus was often depicted as a young man (or child) with wings and a bow, and is often mistaken for Cupid, or Eros. He is also the twin brother of the god of death, Thanatos. As a child of Nyx, he is often said to resident in the underworld, or even Tartarus, but according to the great scribe Homer, he also lived on the island of Lemnos. It was said that the river Lethe flowed through his underworld home. The river Lethe was one of the main rivers in the underworld, and had the power -- as often seen in various myths and stories --- to take away a person's memory. Also present in his abode underground were various types of flowers, and quite a number of hallucinogenic herbs as well. In other words, Somnus had all sorts of means to achieve deep sleep, or at least a catatonic state; the condition of dreams. He himself had three sons -- Morpheus, Icelus, and Phantasus -- all of them gods of various dreams (of men, of animals, and of inanimate objects, respectively, all inhabiting the dream world). In book 14 of Homer's *Iliad*, Juno asked for Somnus' help to put her husband, Jupiter, the king of the gods, to sleep. She wished to help the Greeks win their war with Troy, but Jupiter had been adamant that there was to be no divine intervention in the conflict. The stakes were too high, and various gods were on one side or another, making intervention dangerous not only on earth, but on Olympus as well. Though the plotting pair was eventually discovered by Jupiter, and they were subsequently forced into hiding, Nyx gave Somnus shelter in her home, knowing that Jupiter would not dare follow him into his mother's subterranean cave. Despite their failure, Juno thanked Somnus for his services by giving him a wife, who was named Pasithea. One of Somnus' more famous powers was the ability to put mortals and immortals alike into a deep and possibly permanent sleep, thus making him fairly dangerous, even to someone as powerful as the king of the gods himself. For this reason Somnus, though not considered a major god, was still an important one, and a being who figured prominently in the tales of the ancient world.

Tellus
Temple of Tellus
Rome, Italy
268 BCE

Tellus mater or Terra mater (meaning mother-earth) was the goddess of the earth. During the imperial era, Tellus and Terra were considered two goddesses, though they were nearly indistinguishable. Tellus was one of the older worshipped goddesses as she was one of the original earth goddesses revered during the Roman Republic, and even earlier than that time. She is often connected with the king of the gods, Jupiter, because of their contrasting domains, sky vs. earth. There is a temple honoring Tellus which was built in 304 BCE, after an earthquake shook Rome during the war with the Picentians. She along with many others has her own festival, which was celebrated annually on April 15th. This festival, called Fordicidia, or Horidicidia, after the Latin words Fordus and Hordus, which meant "the bearing of a cow". This festival included a sacrifice of cows that was offered in the capital by vestal virgins. Another festival that was celebrated in her honor as well as the honor of Ceres, was celebrated January 24-26. During these three days Romans prayed to these two goddesses to protect and encourage the fertility of their crops. Offerings included cakes as well as sows, and plow-oxen. Tellus was also worshipped privately right before harvest time. Moreover, when a family member died, she was also called upon to protect their physical body as well as their soul, seeing as how they were buried in the earth (her domain). Because of her connection to the dead in this way, she was also associated with the underworld and with the earth's surface. The goddess was also known for her marriage to the sky-god Uranus, and she is often depicted with a cornucopia, which symbolized her connection to bounty and plentitude. The famous ancient Roman scholar and author Marcus Varro deemed Tellus as one of the Diselecti, which were the twenty most important gods of Rome, as well as one of about a dozen gods pertaining to agriculture. As one of the principal gods and also as one of the oldest deities, the Romans also considered her a goddess of creation. In this way, her domain stretched into fertility and marriage, as well as earth and agriculture. The Latin word "telluris", from which the name Tellus was derived, meant "land, territory, earth, and ground".

Fides

University of California Libraries
California, USA
1900

Fides is the goddess of trust and good faith, hence the saying "bona fides" in modern English. She was most prevalent in Roman paganism, and was one of the first embodiments of virtue. Fides' job was to hold Romans accountable, a moral compass for society at large. She was also associated with Jupiter, and had a temple next to his on Capitoline Hill that was built in 254 BCE. Sacrifices were always offered to her using covered hands, or a cloth to symbolize the trust between the divine and mortals on earth. For example, during an annual ritual, priests called the "Flamen of Jupiter" would have to cover their right hands, when swearing or taking an oath. A man named Gaius Mucius Scaevola was said to have had his right hand cut off because the cloth fell off his hand while he was swearing an oath, which shows how serious the Romans were about this belief. She was also known as Fide Publica during the latter part of the Roman Empire because she was believed to be the keeper of war treaties and other documents regarding the state. Such important charters were in turn kept in her temple for safe keeping. A multitude of military documents were said to have been hung on the sides of the temple until at least the first century CE. To further emphasize Fides' importance to the empire, the Roman senate would occasionally meet in her temple. She is often depicted as a young woman wearing a veil, which was a symbol of purity, both for her and generally in Roman society. Fides is also often seen holding a cup, an olive branch, and/or a turtle, which symbolized her associations with peace and honesty. She first appeared in the Roman pantheon in the third century CE, though historians believe that a cult worshipped her much earlier, during the reign of Numa, the second king of Rome. Her image was printed on many coins during the reign of Emperor Augustus. Later artists like the late nineteenth and early twentieth century painter Edward Sylvester Eillis also took an interest in her, as the accompanying illustrations shows two thousand years later. It is interesting that we know so little about her despite her obvious importance to the Roman pantheon of gods, as well as the Roman people as a whole.

Hercules as Hero
Capital Line Museum
Rome, Italy
1119-1121

This bust depicts the emperor Commodus dressed up as Hercules, complete with the skin of the Nemean lion, the apples of the Hesperides, and his club. The two figures near his torso show two Tritons. Hercules, a hero in classical mythology, was born a demigod and later turned into a god. As a demigod, his godly parents were the king himself, Jupiter (or Zeus), while his mother was a mortal on Earth, Alcmenea. The equivalent of the Greek hero Heracles, he was known for his strength and incredible quests and adventures, later becoming one of the most well-known demigods in history. However in both of these pictures, it is not Hercules standing there, but actually the emperor Commodus, dressed up as the demigod instead. Commodus was known for his passion for the gladiatorial arts, taking it so far as to join the gladiators himself in the arena, at times dressed as his idol, Hercules. It was not uncommon for people of power (especially emperors at the time) to dress up as renowned heroes, and Hercules was the most often imitated. One could often see people dressed in the stereotypical lion-head cape, while brandishing a spiked club, all in a gesture to Hercules. His strength was admired and feared by all, including the gods themselves, as stories circulated about his fights and encounters with major gods such as Neptune, Mars, and even his father Jupiter himself. Moreover, the twelve labors of Hercules were a series of quests given to him by King Eurystheus of Tiryns. Over the course of twelve long years, he travelled around the world to complete these labors. His first task, as above, was to kill the Nemean lion, a monster whose hide was so impenetrable that it seemed impossible to harm him.

The result of this battle could be seen in trophy-form on his back, with the cape he fashioned out of the lion's hide. The second task was to kill the Lernean Hydra, a snake-like monster whose head, once cut off, would sprout two more heads to replace it. Not only was Hercules known for his brawn, but also for his smarts. As such, he killed the hydra by quickly slicing off all of its heads and using a torch to seal off the wounds, so that the heads could not then grow back. The third labor was to capture Diana's beloved stag, who possessed gold horns. Hercules found this task to be one of the most daunting, as he had to capture the delicate animal without hurting it, or enraging Artemis. However, he finally caught the deer after an entire year, finishing the third quest.

Hercules as Deity
Palazzo Massimo Museum
Rome, Italy
2nd Century AD

The *Testa di Eracle* was originally made separately to be attached to an existing statue. Judging by the angle and facial expressions of the bust, the statue was a representation of Hercules sitting. This remake was inspired by a statue by the Greek sculptor Lysippos of Sicyon, *Herakles Epitrapezios*. Though born a demi-god, after his life of heroism the gods made Hercules himself into a God. Though much to his dismay, and (later) one of his many causes of his characteristic bitterness, Hercules became a minor god, and was cast by his father Jupiter to be the guardian (though in his view, lowly door-keeper) of the entrance of the Mare Nostrum. As a god, though he could appear in many different places at once, he was tied to his duty at this post. Hercules was stationed on an island at the entrance of the Mare Nostrum, the encircling (but also dangerous) sea of the Roman empire. This was to some extent a forbidden space. However, Hercules was extremely disheartened by this task, which he viewed as the job of a servant. This was not worthy of his renown and talent. He also viewed this as a punishment of sorts, because he was isolated on an island with one of his old mortal enemies, Achelous (who was half bull and half man). A river god from Aetolia, Achelous was worshipped as the god of fresh water, generally. The story is told of Hercules and Achelous both vying for the hand of an Aetolian princess named Deianeira. During their battle for her affection, Hercules tore off one of Achelous' horns, which had the power to spew out fresh water and various types of food. This horn became known as the horn of plenty, or the first cornucopia. Hercules ended up winning the match and won Deianeria's hand in marriage. With a horn severed from his head, much of Achelous' original power was diminished. Because Hercules was always away on voyages, and was known for being a womanizer, Dianeira was constantly worried about his fidelity, and was often jealous as a result. When a trickster satyr heard of her dilemma, he drove Dianeieria into a crazed state of mind, and influenced her to poison one of her husband's garments. When Hercules returned home and put on the garment, he died. Deianeira, realizing what she had done, killed herself to be with her husband. However, unbeknownst to her, he was then later resurrected again by the gods. So while both Hercules and Aechelus were on this small island, they tried to stay out of each other's way. However, the love and regret regarding the life and death of Deianeira could be felt -- spanning the distance between them.

Nyx
Watercolor
Gustave Moreau
1880

Nyx was the goddess of the night, and one of the oldest goddesses in the Roman pantheon. She was called a primordial god, meaning that she was born at the beginning of time. Nyx was considered neither a good nor a bad deity, as the night could bring either sleep or death, one of these a good outcome of closing one's eyes, the other one, not so good. She was considered a very powerful goddess especially since Jupiter himself, the king of the gods, was fearful only of her. The moonstone is her symbol, as it reflects her personality (and moon light). Nyx was said to have lived in Tartarus, the deepest and darkest part of the underworld, a palace where souls were tormented (essentially, the ancient version of Hell). Though she was often considered evil because of her domain and her dwelling, she never actually committed any evil acts that we know about. Despite her age and power, she was not considered a major god, and was not worshipped as such. The goddess married Erebus, the god of darkness, and together they had many children, including Hemera, the goddess of the day, and Aither, the goddess of light. These two children were particularly notable because of their striking contrast to their parents. Nyx and Erebus had created other dark spirits, however, including the Fates, Sleep, Death, Strife, Pain, as well as Nemesis. Though as above she was not considered a central deity, she was mentioned in various mythologies, including one that occurred between one of her sons, Somnus, the god of sleep, and Jupiter. The tale says that Jupiter's wife, Juno, had asked Somnus to use his power to put Jupiter asleep, while she plotted against him. Unfortunately, the plan did not work, and Jupiter found out what Juno and Somnus were trying to do. Jupiter was rightfully furious, and started hunting down Somnus. Nyx heard about her son's encounter with the king of the gods, and offered him refuge in her cave in Tartarus. As the sole being whom Jupiter feared, Somnus was protected, and Jupiter eventually retreated. Nyx was always portrayed as a beautiful woman shrouded in darkness and mist, and accompanied by one of her numerous children. The darkness that surrounded her was supposedly her husband, Erebus, and this is portrayed in many images of her as well.

Venti
Duke University Libraries
Durham, North Carolina
1721

The Anemoi were the gods of the four winds. Boreas controlled the north wind; Zephryos controlled the west; Notos controlled the south, and Euros the east wind. With these four gods came also the associated seasons: Boreas manifested the winter; Zephryos the spring; Notos the summer, and Euros the Autumn. These four gods were often depicted as winged men, or as horses. The distinction between the four was made early on by famous poets such as Homer. The Venti were also affiliated with the Harpies, who were viewed as their female counterparts. Moreover, many stories detail how the Harpies and the Venti would mate to produce immortal horses, faster than any other horses in the Ancient World. These divine tempests also had a sanctuary that was built in 259 BCE, at the Porta Capena, in Rome. This temple was founded after a vow was made to protect a Roman fleet at sea during a particularly bad storm. Roman generals would always pray to these wind gods as well as give them offerings and sacrifices before embarking on a sea-faring trip. The four wind gods were so distinct in fact that Romans would offer white animals to the warm winds, while darker colored animals were offered to the cold winds. The most common sacrificial animals were rams and lambs. When described as the four horses, the gods were the manifestations of the more powerful storm god Aeolus. A famous story was in the Odyssey, when Aeolus gave Odysseus free reign of these four horses/gods to make his travels faster across the Mediterranean. According to the famous Greek poet Hesiod, the parents of the Venti were Aeolus and the goddess of the dawn, Eos. Boreas, being the harbinger of the cold north wind, was always depicted as having a violent temper, and was closely associated with Athenians. Zephyros, the god of the west wind, was known as the most gentle of the four, and as the messenger of Spring. Notos brought about hot wind, and was the most feared, because of his reputation as the destroyer of crops. Finally Euros was believed to be the unlucky east wind, though he brought warmth and rain, which the Romans prized and appreciated. Though these four were the major wind gods, there were also minor wind gods and offspring of these gods who had lesser functions, when it came to the atmosphere.

Apollo
Palazzo Massimo Museum
Rome, Italy
2nd Century AD

This particular statue of Apollo, the *Apollo Tipo Anzio,* portrays the god in an ambiguous and polymorphic nature, emphasized by its feminine appearance and hairstyle. Without the presence of the snake, one of Apollo's most famous hallmarks, the statue might not have even been identified as the god Apollo. As the patron of the sun, light, music and prophecy, as well as art, poetry, archery, and medicine, Apollo was a very complex and useful god. He is the twin brother of the goddess Diana, and the son of Jupiter and a titan named Leto. When Jupiter's wife Juno found out that Jupiter had cheated on her once again, and that Leto was bearing two children, she traveled down to the mortal realm and made all of the midwives promise that they would not help Leto give birth. When she was turned away by midwives from all corners of the earth, Leto finally came upon the small island of Delos, which Juno had missed because Delos was a small, unobtrusive islet. After much anguish, Leto finally birthed the two twins, Diana and Apollo, and in this miraculous event, rooted the small island to the earth. Apollo himself is often characterized by his youthful athletic appearance, and was known for his charm and good looks. He was also associated with the Delphic oracle, and could on occasion predict prophecy. Another area of his association was medicine, and healing in general, however expertise in this field was granted to Apollo's immortal son, Asclepius. The staff of Asclepius is the most recognized symbol of medicine today. Apollo is one of the few gods whose name did not change in moving from Greek civilization to Roman civilization. The most significant difference between his Greek and Roman identities was that the Romans considered Apollo more of a god of healing and prophecy, while the Greeks considered Apollo to be the god of the sun. A famous fable regarding Apollo was when he accidentally killed his lover, Hyacinthus. Another immortal god, Eros, son of Venus, was also in love with Hyacinthus, and during a game of discus, Eros out of jealousy, shifted the winds so that the discus that Apollo had thrown ended up hitting Hyacinthus' head, killing him. When Apollo realized what he had done, he used his power to create the first Hyacinth flower from his lover's remains. This fragrant, spring-blooming flower can be almost all colors of the rainbow, and are still seen today.

Mercury

British Museum
London, England
Roman 1st century CE copy of Greek original 330-300 BCE

Here, Mercury (or his Greek parallel, Hermes) stands in a calm, relaxed pose, inadvertently showing off his athletic figure -- which exhibits the ideal physique of a god. Many different versions of this statue are preserved and exhibited around the world, especially in the Mediterranean. This particular statue was restored during the Renaissance, when it was first discovered and was given new arms and a left leg. The decorated base can be traced back to about 300-100 BCE. Like his Greek counterpart, Mercury was born to be the god of commerce. Serving as the middleman between the divine and mortals, Mercury's winged shoes gave him the advantage of speed. With this, his patronage included travelers, merchants, as well as thieves, and even tricksters. The god was also characterized by his winged hat, and his staff (caduceus). This staff was known to have two snakes intertwined on it, and was often mistaken for the symbol of medicine, the staff of Asclepius. As a son of the king of gods (Jupiter), Mercury was also considered one of the "Big Twelve", the most important of the gods. Though most famous as the god of commerce, Mercury was also the patron of cheating and thievery, and was a master-thief himself. Mythology often recalls his child-like nature, and his pranks on the other gods, especially his half-brother Apollo. Moreover, Mercury was the only god who was free to travel to the underworld at his leisure, other than Pluto himself. This was because he was also responsible for bringing the souls of the dead there. As the chief messenger of the gods, it was his duty to be swift and sure, as well as knowledgeable of all events. Much like many other gods, he was known to have female as well as male lovers, the most famous being the Greek hero Perseus. The god was also known for assisting Ceres and Jupiter in their famous search for Persephone (Proserpina), when she was kidnapped by Pluto, the god of the Underworld. Ceres enlisted the help of Mercury as the god of communications and travel, and he eventually found Proserpina with Pluto in the Underworld. Mercury was the one who escorted her out of the underworld and back home to her mother in the land of the living. Another famous tale of his thieving nature occurred when Mercury tried to steal cattle from his brother Apollo. When Jupiter was requested to settle the feud, Mercury brought with him a string instrument, the first-ever lyre. Knowing Apollo would take interest in it as the god of music, he exchanged the lyre for the cattle, eventually settling the situation.

Asclepius

Rijksmuseum
Amsterdam, Netherlands
1602-1607

Asclepius is the Roman god of medicine, and is also known as Asclepius, or the Vejove. He is the son of Apollo, the god of the sun, among other attributes (prophecy, art, poetry, music) and Coronis, a mortal princess. He and his wife Epione, who was the goddess of tranquility and comfort, had many children, including Panacea, Hygeia, Iaso, and others. Two of their sons, named Machaon and Podalirius, were known during the Trojan War as talented healers, which was fitting given their parentage. Asclepius was born a demi-god, so he was brought to the famous demi-god trainer, a centaur named Chiron. Chiron had raised and trained many heroes before him, including Hercules and Achilles, and taught Asclepius everything he knew about medicine and healing. Though Chiron knew much about medicine, it was actually a snake that Asclepius had healed that taught him the secrets of the field. In ancient times, snakes were considered healing animals that were both divine and cunning. This is how the symbol of Asclepius later became a snake wrapped around a rod. This symbol is especially important as it is very much still relevant in modern culture, and in fact is still the symbol of medicine today. Many hospitals not only have Asclepius' rod on their buildings and next to their company names, but it is also a general symbol in modern Western culture for the idea of medicine. Given that he was born a demi-god, he possessed certain healing powers, but he did not reach full divine status until Jupiter, the king of the gods, realized that one of his many talents was cheating death and bringing mortals back from the brink of death. Different myths recount different events regarding Jupiter's reaction. One was that

Jupiter ended up killing Asclepius to preserve the natural balance of life. Another tale said that Jupiter simply banished Asclepius to an isolated cave where he was forbidden to practice any medicine that could result in the avoidance of death for mortals. Roman medicine was quite advanced for its time in the ancient world, and because of this, Asclepius was seen as an important god. Also, the Romans were involved in so much warfare that a god with his talents was seen as necessary. Roman medicine spread throughout the empire from Rome out toward the rest of the conquered world.

Pan
Palazzo Massimo Museum
Rome, Italy
Early Imperial Period

This figure can be identified as the god of the wild, Pan. While the structure has since been recovered, many parts of the statue have not yet been found, leading professionals to believe that the original sculpture must have been completed with a *pedum* (curved shepherd's crook) in the right hand and a *syrinx* (*Pan's pipes)* in the other. Pan is one of the lesser-known gods, as he was a patron of a more spiritual world, as well as being not very Roman (Romans did love their violence). Although he was a minor god, he is often referenced in historical mythology as one of the oldest gods. People who worshipped Pan were usually not people who lived in big cities, where forests and pasture lands were not well-represented. As the patron of shepherds, hunters, and woodland music, Pan is often depicted in the company of nymphs and spirits who resided in his domain. While most gods and goddesses could transform and shift into various animals and other guises, the god Pan was often portrayed as a satyr, a man with the legs of a goat and the upper body of a human male, with horns on his head. His Roman name was Faunus, but Greeks and Romans alike most often referred to him as Pan. Mythological stories featuring Pan often tell of his gentle nature, and his unusual appearance. His talents included his ability to play reed pipes, which was later named the "pan flute". One of his stories involves a wood nymph named Syrinx. After repeatedly rejecting Pan's affections, she ran away to a river, and called upon the goddesses to turn her into a reed, so that she could hide from the pursuing god. When Pan arrived at the field of reeds next to the river, he could not distinguish which of the reeds was her. In his frustration, he cut down several reeds, and laid them in a line, forming his first reed-pipes, which even now are still associated with him. It was said that his musical talents along with his patronage of the forest allowed him to use his pipes as an extension of his power, much like Jupiter and his lightning bolts, or Neptune and his trident. He could will various plants to grow quickly, and he was also associated with parties and merry-making. The most famous story of Pan involved the god crying out the word "panic" to a mass of his enemies in the midst of a war, which, given his power, caused uncontrollable fear in his opponents. Pan was beloved in both Greece and Rome, and more than many other gods, really straddled both cultures as an important figure in the mythological pantheon.

Cloacina

Provenance: Rome Mint
Silver Denarius Coin
42 BCE

Cloacina "The Cleanser" was the goddess of the sewers of Rome. The Latin verb "to cleanse" was Cluo, and it was from this verb that her name was derived. Cloaca means "drain" or "sewer". Being a goddess of the sewers meant that she also symbolized filth as well as purification and cleanliness, a paradoxical state of affairs. Though she was not considered a major goddess and was never mentioned alongside major deities, like Minerva and Mars, she was vitally important to Roman life. It is unusual that a civilization (ancient or otherwise) would recognize and respect a god whose function was dealing with the disposal of waste. Cloacina can be traced back to Etruscan times, and was later adopted by the Romans. She was believed to reside around the Cloaca Maxima (the greatest sewer drain in the city of Rome itself, which was where all the sewers connected, in one central hub). Much like bath-houses being famously connected to Roman culture, so too were the advanced aqueducts of Rome equally-famous. Such a system was vitally important to the success of the city, given the constant risks of disease, flooding and infestations. This was because Roma's water-ways were crucial to the city's life, and brought water from very far away into the city itself. Modern sewer systems have been modeled after such ancient examples of engineering for hundreds upon hundreds of years. Some of the aqueducts of Rome still stand, which is a testament to their architectural strength and innovation. Though Cloacina was considered to have an unglamorous domain, she was still worshipped and venerated and treated with much respect. In terms of artworks, Cloacina was depicted in both statues and in shrines. The most famous shrine was the Sacrum Cloacina, a place which was said to lead to the sewers beneath the city. This sanctum built in her honor still has visible foundations that can be seen today by tourists and visitors to Rome, as part of the Forum. The most common offering to Cloacina was (perhaps not surprisingly) incense, given its practical application for dealing with foul-smelling air around sewers, drains and latrines. Much like this example, her face was also commemorated on Roman coins, which were often used to toss into magnificent fountains, around the city of Rome. The contrast between this and her place in the sewers is really quite interesting. We actually have Cloacina to thank for modern plumbing.

Janus
Provenance: Roman Mint
Issued by C. Fabius Hadrianus
102 BCE

This is an extremely rare coin with only five known examples extant in the world. The coin was issued by C. Fabius Hadrianus in 102 BC, and shows the Roman god Janus alongside a Roman shop, and a stork (a sea-bird). Janus was the god of choices and transitions and was usually depicted (as shown here) as having two faces looking in opposite directions. The left face was supposed to represent the past, while the one facing right represented the future. Though many deities were brought over from the Greek mythological tradition through assimilation, Janus is unique in that he has no Greek equivalent. In Roman mythology he was considered one of the most important gods, as his domain consisted of abstract ideas such as time, motion, and transitions in general. It is said that he was one of the oldest gods, and that he was present at the birth of the world. His age also made people think he was a part of the process and birth of religion, and of life itself on earth. As the guardian of the gates to Heaven, many Romans would first mention his name in prayer, so as to reach the gods to whom they were praying. One of the most famous stories regarding Janus involved one of the founders of Rome itself, Romulus. It is said that when Romulus and his men kidnapped the Sabine women, Janus rescued them by demonstrating his power and creating an active volcano which erupted and killed the kidnappers. As a patron of transitional periods in general, he was especially important in times of war, and subsequently, in peace. Even before the formation of the Capitoline triad, Roman religions were founded on the idea of family and the household. As such, spirits (or Numina) represented or inhabited everything within a house. The most important of these spirits included Vesta, the spirit of the hearth; Penates, the spirits of the kitchen; Lar Familiarus, the guardian of the family fortune and cultivated land; and finally Janus, the spirit of doorways. As such, so as to not anger or disrespect these spirits, small portions of every meal were offered to these spirits. These domestic deities would eventually be incorporated into Gods of the Roman state religion, and would be found all throughout the empire. Janus did not have the awesome outward power of many of the other principle gods, but because of his association with the household, he was found literally everywhere, and was respected and revered accordingly.

Luna
British Museum
London, England
1st century CE

This bronze lamp represents Luna, the roman goddess of the moon. She was also commonly known as Selene in Graeco-Roman religion. As one of many moon goddesses, she was most worshipped during new and full moons. Though she was considered a goddess, her parents were Titans, Hyperion and Theia. Because of her parentage, she is considered one of few deities who preceded the Olympian pantheon. She also had multiple siblings, including Helios, the god of the sun, and Eos, the goddess of the dawn. She is mentioned in many famous mythologies, including "Hymn to Selene" by Homer. She is associated with a mortal man named Endymion, who was said to have been her lover. Unfortunately, Jupiter cast Endymion into an eternal sleep and forced Luna to visit him on Mount Latmus. It is also said that the pair had given birth to fifty daughters. In other stories, it is said that she was loved by the god of nature and wildlife, Pan. Luna is also often mistaken for Diana, the most famous of the various moon goddesses. However, though there were many moon goddesses, she was the only one that was truly the embodiment of the moon itself. She is often depicted as a woman driving a chariot pulled by two horses across the sky. It is said that this chariot was the moon being dragged across the heavens. Moreover, most artworks featuring the goddess feature a crescent-shaped crown or symbol atop her head. In paintings especially Luna often had a while halo or radiance glowing around her, which symbolized her beauty and affinity to the brightness of the moon. Luna was also commemorated with temples on both the Aventine and Palatine hills in Rome. Much like many other deities during this time, a cult formed that worshipped her specifically. The formation of this cult further proved Luna's origins in ancient shamanistic rituals. A famous mythological creature that is associated with Lua is the Nemean lion, who is said to have spring from the moon. After birth the lion was cared for and nurtured by Luna in a cave, where she discovered that his hide was impenetrable. Another symbol of Luna was the bull, so when Ampelos, the mortal lover of Bacchus, boldly challenged Luna while riding a bull, the goddess taught him a lesson by making the bull buck under him. The bull then threw Ampelos onto the ground and impaled him with his horns.

Bronze lamp representing goddess Luna

Cupid
Palazzo Massimo Museum
Rome, Italy
2 CE

This fresco depicts dolphins swimming in the ocean, with a young Cupid riding on one of its backs. The painting features several fish casting shadows in the water. For the most part, the sea animals shown represented species that lived by the ocean, or were specifically bred by the Romans in ponds. Cupid was the Roman god of love and desire. His Greek parallel was named Eros. The role of this god changed over time with the presence of Christian influence in the Roman empire. Cupid was originally portrayed as a small boy with wings, but became known as a chubby child with a bow and arrow -- this remains his symbol to this day. His bow and arrow could make any mortal or immortal fall in love. According to mythology, Cupid possessed two different arrows. The golden arrow represented true love, while the leaden arrow represented sensual desire alone. The existence of these two arrows goes to show why cupid is associated with any and all types of love. The most famous story involving Cupid was his encounter with the beautiful mortal named Psyche. Psyche was the youngest daughter of a king but she rivalled the beauty of the goddess of love, Venus. When Venus heard of Psyche's reputation, she became jealous, and asked her son, Cupid, to shoot the mortal with an arrow, to fall in love with a monster. Because Cupid himself had never fallen in love, he thought nothing of the task. However, when face to face with Psyche, he realized her true beauty, and while attempting to shoot an arrow at her, he became flustered, and accidentally shot himself in the foot. This mistake led to the inevitable infatuation that Cupid had with the mortal. Psyche was whisked away by the west wind to a beautiful palace with everything she could ever want, including invisible servants, etc. When Cupid finally introduced himself to her, he told her that he would only visit at night, when she could not look upon his divine face. Psyche was confused by Cupid's beautiful voice, and wondered why he was keeping his face from her. As days went by, she became homesick and lonely, and eventually called her sisters to visit. Jealous of her palace and riches, her sisters convinced Psyche that she must look at her new husband. They convinced her that he was the fabled monster that she had been fated to fall in love with, and that the only way she could outrun her fate was to kill him. Psyche used a candle and a knife to illuminate Cupid's sleeping face, but was surprised by how handsome he was. However, Cupid instantly woke up, and disappeared in a cloud of smoke. Furious with his wife, and telling her that she would now never see him again, he disappeared forever.

Moses
Pantheon
Rome, Italy
Date Unknown

Moses was a religious figure of deep importance to Jews in the Roman empire. As with Christian populations, Jews were a minority who were often mistreated by their Roman masters. Jews lived in many parts of the empire but were particularly found in Judea, or what is today Israel, Jordan, and Palestine. Unlike Christianity, Judaism actually predated the rise of Rome as a religion. Jews were incorporated into the Roman empire as traders and in other occupations, so they were often considered useful. However, they also rebelled against Roman rule in several instances, most famously at Masada in the Holy Land, in 70 A.D. Moses was seen as a savior for Jews. He had, in the Old Testament, led his people out of Egypt, and God had parted the waters to allow their escape from bondage. Moses was similarly seen in Roman times as a symbol of freedom by Jewish populations. His image was carved by sculptors, both Jewish and non-Jewish, in Roman times and for centuries afterwards. In later centuries, some sculptors gave him horns, multiplying the notion that he was connected to the devil. Michelangelo sculpted perhaps the most famous image of Moses during the Renaissance, a statue that is still visited by millions in our own time. Moses was a heroic figure for Jewish populations, in that he symbolized the possibility of action, as Jews usually lived under the rule of others, and therefore remained in their power. The impact of statuary depicting Moses therefore, had different meanings depending on the viewer: for some he symbolized freedom, and for others, he symbolized rebellion. The most famous story regarding his heroism in saving his people from tyranny, happened in Egypt, where he declared to the pharaoh that he was going to free all of the Jews from bondage. He warned the pharaoh that if he did not let the Israelites go in peace, God would send numerous waves of plagues to show his displeasure of the ruler's actions. Sure enough, after the pharaoh scoffed at his proclamation, 10 plagues descended onto the Egyptians. These plagues included water turning to blood, frogs, lice, flies, livestock pestilence, boils, hail, locusts, darkness, and the killing of firstborn children. He became known as the Hebrew Prophet, and when he led the Jews out of Egypt and out of enslavement, he cemented his connections with the divine when God parted the Red Sea for the Jews to pass.

Jesus
Pantheon
Rome, Italy
Date Unknown

Jesus was worshipped by a new sect that appeared in the Roman empire around the year 0 -- that of Christianity. This was a minority group who left the gods of Rome to worship this new prophet, who preached a doctrine of love and service to one's fellow man. Christians were persecuted by the Romans, including being fed to lions, and being forced to participate in gladiatorial games. The word of Christianity spread through the so-called disciples of Christ, men like Peter, Paul, and others who would become known later as saints. Christianity spread to all corners of the empire, and eventually throughout the world to become the most practiced religion on Earth. But the epicenter of Christianity in early Roman times was the Holy Land, or what is today Israel, Jordan, and Palestine. Jesus' message of compassion and love stood in stark contrast to the very authoritarian principles of Roman rule. Romans also had a huge number of gods, each with a different purpose and specialty. By combining all of these attributes of devotion into one person, Christians simplified their spiritual lives, and focused their piety on a single figure. Christians were ruthlessly hunted as the religion grew in popularity after Jesus' death. His crucifixion, on a hill in present day Israel, became a focal point for the maintenance of the faith for Christians worldwide. Eventually, the Roman empire itself adopted Christianity, when its decline occurred in the early centuries of the first millennium. Now, the Vatican City, in the northern parts of the city of Rome, is the center of global Christianity, right in the heart of the old Roman empire. Because of the constant persecution, Christianity was often practiced in secret, often in underground churches scattered around the Roman Empire. At the very beginnings of the religion, nonbelievers assumed that Jesus would simply be another deity to add to the long list of worshipped gods. When it became apparent that Christianity was a monotheistic religion, Roman emperors revolted, believing that people having a sole focus of worship would undermine their authority and endanger the unity of the empire. The eventual adoption of Christianity by segments of the general Roman population in the early centuries CE started the lasting shift from traditional Graeco-Roman gods to a new monotheistic religion. This shift was made possible by the efforts of a famous Roman emperor named Constantine, who led his people into the new religion by converting himself in 312 CE.

Saint Sebastian
Saint Agnes Church
Rome, Italy
1717-1719

Saint Sebastian was a Christian martyr who lived in the third-century CE. Before converting to Christianity, he was a soldier in Diocletian's army. There, he converted many soldiers and took advantage of his military position by helping Christians in prison. When discovered in the year 286 CE, he was sentenced to death and was tied to a column and pierced with arrows. Thinking he was dead, the guards left him to be buried, but Sebastian was rescued and nursed back to health by a woman named Irene, whose Christian husband was a servant of Diocletian and was later martyred as well. After regaining his strength, Sebastian bravely faced Diocletian again, publicly criticizing him for his persecution of Christians. Diocletian then ordered him to be beaten and thrown into the sewers. The statue depicts Sebastian tied to the column and being pierced by arrows- the time of his martyrdom. There are four different arrows piercing him in his chest, shoulder, back, and leg. His body seems to be contorting inwards from the pain of being stabbed. Crossing an emperor was not something that was done lightly; the fact that he survived the arrows made him destined to have to endure a more gruesome death in the sewers. There is a gold version of the Christian cross in front of the statue; its beams of golden light mimic the movement of the golden arrows. Sculpted by Pietro Paolo Campi between 1717 and 1719, this statue is exhibited in the Saint Agnes Church in Rome, right across from a statue of Saint Agnes herself. The two statues are actually similar in style and decoration, courtesy of the famous architect, Francesco Borromini. All of the colors present at this site indicate a divine presence to the viewer: the blue sky, the sunset clouds, the golden cross -- all point to an idealized scene. The statue displays a common characteristic of post-Renaissance art -- a maintenance of traditionally idealized figures and unrealistic shapes and proportions of the human body. But it also shows the humanistic idea of the importance of man and his potential value and goodness, all depicted here in the body of Saint Sebastian. The image of Saint Sebastian being pierced by golden arrows is iconic within Christianity. He symbolized the devotion to faith in spite of great personal suffering, and was an important figure of the sainthood of the religion. He is most commonly known for his patronage of athletes and soldiers, along with anyone that wanted to die a saint.

Saint Emerenziana (Christian Sister of St. Agnes)
Saint Agnes Church
Rome, Italy
4th century CE

Saint Emerenziana lived in the fourth century after Christ and died in 304 CE. She was the foster sister of Saint Agnes in which this church was dedicated. Her mother was the wet-nurse and nanny of Saint Agnus, so the two girls were raised together, and had a common mother-figure in their lives. Emerenziana died tragically at the early age of twelve after being stoned to death by the order of Diocletian after having been discovered commemorating her sister's grave. She was also bravely opposing a group of pagans, who were trying to halt the funeral of her sister (Saint Agnes). In this piece, Saint Emerenziana is shown standing in front of her sister's grave, while her sister shows her Heaven. The statue was sculpted by two artists -- Ercole Ferrata, who died only having finished the lower portion of the frieze, and Leonardo Retti, who completed the Ferrata's work. We see here a very clear narrative of the story of Saint Emerenziana. This was typical of the school of Alessandro Algardi. The man who started the sculpture, Ferrata, was considered to be Algardi's best student. The frieze is enormous, and has many figures all in motion at the same time, in various poses. We also get a sense of the verticality of heaven over Earth, in the top-down nature of the sculpture. One can tell that it is heaven that Saint Emerenziana is headed towards by the intricate folds and ruffles of the upper-left portion of the frieze, made to look like the clouds on which rests the city. One can feel the movement of many bodies in motion of this sculptural frieze, as all four corners have figures in action. The amount of detail that is shown can be seen in the many curls of hair, and the infinite amount of flowing layers of the figures' robes. One can also tell that this frieze was dedicated to Saint Emerenziana by the way all of the other figures have their bodies and heads angled toward Emerenziana, drawing one's eyes to the center of the piece, where a woman wrapped in cloth looks up into the heavens. Saint Emerenziana has an official feast day of January 23rd every year; this date has existed for such celebrations for a very long time now, and into the present. She is usually depicted as a young girl, with rocks in her lap representing the manner in which she died, and lilies in her hand. Her tomb lies in the church of Saint Agnes in central Rome, where she can still be visited by those adoring her, and her sense of sacrifice.

Augustus	27 B.C.-14 A.D.	Aurelian	270-275
Tiberius	14-37	Tacitus	275-276
Caligula	37-41	Florian	276
Claudius	41-54	Probus	276-282
Nero	54-68	Carus	282-283
Galba	68-69	Carinus	283-285
Otho	69	Diocletian	284-305
Vitellius	69	Maximian	286-305
Vespasian	69-79	Constantine, Licinius	307-324
Titus	79-81	Constantine	324-337
Domitian	81-96	Julian the Apostate	360-363
Nerva	96-98	Valentinian I	364-375
Trajan	98-117	Valens	364-378
Hadrian	117-138	Theodosius I	378-395
Antoninus Pius	138-161	Honorius	395-423
Marcus Aurelius	161-180	Arcadius (E)	395-408
Lucius Verus	161-169	Theodosius II (E)	408-450
Commodus	180-192	Valentinian III	425-455
Pertinax	193	Marcian (E)	450-457
Didius Julianus	193	Maximus	455
Septimius Severus	193-211	Avitus	455-456
Caracalla	211-217	Leo I (E)	457-474
Geta	211-212	Majorian	457-461
Macrinus	217-218	Severus	461-465
Elagabalus	218-222	Anthemius	467-472
Severus Alexander	222-235	Olybrius	472
Maximinus	235-238	Glycerius	473-474
Gordians I, II, III	238-244	Nepos	474-475
Philip the Arab	244-249	Zeno (E)	474-491
Decius	249-251	Romulus Augustulus	475-476
Valerian	253-260	Anastatius (E)	491-518
Gallienus	253-268	Justin I (E)	518-527
Claudius Gothicus	268-270	Justinian (E)	527-565

Figure 3: Roman Emperor Timeline

Works Consulted and Further Reading:

Anderson, Graham, *Fairytale in the Ancient World* (New York: Routledge 2000).

Ando, C. *The Matter of the Gods.* (Berkeley: University of California Press, 2008).

Ando, C., ed.. *Roman Religion.* (Edinburgh: Edinburgh University Press, 2003).

Beard, M. "Writing and Religion: *Ancient Literacy* and the Function of the Written Word in Roman Religion." *Literacy in the Ancient World.* JRA Supplement 3. (Ann Arbor, MI: Journal of Roman Archaeology, 1991). 35-58.

Beard, M. and J. North eds. *Pagan Priests: Religion and Power in the Ancient World* (Ithaca, N.Y.: Cornell University Press, 1990).

Beard, M., J. North, and S. Price. *Religions of Rome* (Cambridge: Cambridge University Press, 1998). 2 volumes.

Bell, Robert E. *Women in Classical Mythology* (Oxford 1993).

Bernabé, A. and A Jiménez San Cristóbal, *Instructions for the Netherworld: The Orphic Gold Tablets* (Leiden-Boston: Brill 2008).

Brumble, H. David *Classical Myths and Legends in the Middle Ages and Renaissance* (New York Routledge 1998).

Burkert, Walter *Ancient Mystery Cults* (Cambridge: Harvard 1987).

Deacey, Susan *Athena* (New York: Routledge 2008).

Derks, T. *Gods, Temples, and Ritual Practices: The Transformation of Religious Ideas and Values in Roman Gaul.* (Amsterdam: Amsterdam University Press, 1998).

Dougherty, Carol *Prometheus* (New York: Routledge 2005).

Dowden, Ken, *Zeus* (New York Routledge 2005).

Dumézil, G. *Archaic Roman Religion* (Chicago: University of Chicago Press, 1970).

Feeney, D. *Literature and Religion at Rome.* (Cambridge: Cambridge University Press, 1998).

Ferguson, J. *Greek and Roman Religion: A Source Book* (Park Ridge: Noyes Press, 1980).

Fishwick, D. *The Imperial Cult in the Latin West: Studies in the Ruler Cult of the Western Provinces of the Roman Empire.* 8 volumes in 3. (Leiden: E.J. Brill, 1987-2005).

Frankfurter, D. *Religion in Roman Egypt: Assimilation and Resistance.* (Princeton: Princeton University Press, 1998).

Freedman, Luba *The Revival of the Olympian Gods in Renaissance Art* (Cambridge: Cambridge University Press, 2003).

Gradel, I. *Emperor Worship and Roman Religion.* (Oxford: Clarendon Press, 2002).

Graf, Fritz *Apollo* (New York: Routledge 2008).

Grant, Michael *Roman Myths* (New York: Scribners 1971).

Grant, Michael *The Myths of the Greeks and Romans* (New York: NAL-Mentor 1962).

Lefkowitz, Mary *Greek Gods, Human Lives: What We Can Learn From Myths* (New Haven: Yale 2003).

MacMullen, R. *Christianizing the Roman Empire* (New Haven: Yale University Press, 1984).

MacMullen, R. *Paganism in the Roman Empire* (New Haven: Yale University Press, 1981).

Michels, A. K. *The Calendar of the Roman Republic* (Princeton: Princeton University Press, 1967).

Mikalson, Jon D. *Athenian Popular Religion* (Chapel Hill: U. North Carolina 1983).

Nock, A. D. *Essays on Religion and the Ancient World.* Edited by Z. Stewart. (Oxford: Clarendon Press, 1972).

North, J. *Roman Religion* (Oxford: Oxford University Press, 2000).

Ogden, D. *Magic, Witchcraft, and Ghosts in the Greek and Roman Worlds: A Sourcebook.* (2002).

Orlin, E. M. *Temples, Religion and Politics in the Roman Republic* (Leiden: E.J. Brill, 1997).

Page, L. *Folktakes in Homer's Odyssey* (The Carl Newell Jackson Lectures 1972).

Parke, H. W. *Sibyls and Sibylline Prophecy in Classical Antiquity* (New York: Routledge, 1988).

Perowne, Stewart *Roman Mythology* (New York: Paul Hamlyn 1969).

Price, Simon and Emily Kearns (ed.), *The Oxford Dictionary of Classical Myth and Religion* (Oxford: Oxford University Press, 2004).

Rives, J. B. *Religion in the Roman Empire* (Malden, MA: Blackwell, 2007).

Rüpke, J. *Religion of the Romans*. Translated and edited by Richard Gordon (Malden, MA: Polity, 2007).

Rüpke, J., ed. *A Companion to Roman Religion* (Oxford: Blackwell, 2007).

Scheid, J. *An Introduction to Roman Religion*. Translated by Janet Lloyd. Edinburgh: Edinburgh University Press, 2003).

Scheid, J. "The Priest." A. Giardina, ed. *The Romans*. L. G. Cochrane, trans. (Chicago: University of Chicago Press, 1993): 55-84.

Scullard, H. H. *Festivals and Ceremonies of the Roman Republic* (Ithaca, N.Y.: Cornell University Press, 1981).

Seaford, Richard *Dionysos* (New York: Routledge 2006).

Stanford, W.B., and Luce, T.J. *The Quest for Ulysses* (1974).

Taylor, L. R. *Party Politics in the Age of Caesar*. (Berkeley: University of California Press, 1949).

Taylor, L. R. *The Divinity of the Roman Emperor* (Middletown, CT.: American Philological Association, 1931).

Tripp, Edward *The Meridian Handbook of Classical Mythology* (New York: NAL-Meridian 1970).

Turcan, Robert *The Cults of the Roman Empire* (Cambridge: Blackwell 1996 [Paris: Les Belles Lettres 1992]).

Warde Fowler, W. *The Religious Experience of the Roman People, from the Earliest Times to the Age of Augustus* (London: MacMillan, 1911).

Warde Fowler, W. *The Roman Festivals of the Period of the Republic: An Introduction to the Study of the Religion of the Romans*. (London: MacMillan, 1899).

Weinstock, S. *Divus Julius* (Oxford: Clarendon Press, 1971).

Wildfang, Robin L *Rome's Vestal Virgins* (New York: Routledge 2006).

Wiseman, Timothy Peter *Remus: A Roman Myth* (New York: Cambridge University Press, 1995).

Wiseman, Timothy Peter *The Myths of Rome* (Exeter: University of Exeter Press 2004).

Woolf, G. *Becoming Roman: The Origins of Provincial Civilization in Gaul.* (Cambridge: Cambridge University Press, 1998).

Ziolkowski, A. *The Temples of Mid-Republican Rome and Their Historical and Topographical Context.* (Rome: "L'Erma" di Bretschneider, 1992).

www.ingramcontent.com/pod-product-compliance
Ingram Content Group UK Ltd.
Pitfield, Milton Keynes, MK11 3LW, UK
UKHW020247240426
12048UKWH00027B/1650